A LIFE-COACHING APPROACH TO SCREEN ACTING

Lovely to meet you !
Keep going.

A LIFE-COACHING APPROACH TO SCREEN ACTING

DANIEL DRESNER

methuen | drama

LONDON • NEW YORK • OXFORD • NEW DELHI • SYDNEY

METHUEN DRAMA
Bloomsbury Publishing Plc
50 Bedford Square, London, WC1B 3DP, UK
1385 Broadway, New York, NY 10018, USA
29 Earlsfort Terrace, Dublin 2, Ireland

BLOOMSBURY, METHUEN DRAMA and the Methuen Drama logo are trademarks of
Bloomsbury Publishing Plc

First published in Great Britain 2019
Reprinted 2019, 2020, 2021

Cover design: Louise Dugdale
Cover image © Natcha29 / iStock

A catalogue record for this book is available from the British Library.

Library of Congress Cataloging-in-Publication Data
Names: Dresner, Daniel, 1963-author.
Title: A life-coaching approach to screen acting / Daniel Dresner.
Description: London ; New York : Methuen Drama, 2018. |
Includes bibliographical references.
Identifiers: LCCN 2018002428 | ISBN 9781350039421 (hb) | ISBN 9781350039438 (pb) |
ISBN 9781350039414 (ePDF) | ISBN 9781350039445 (eBook)
Subjects: LCSH: Motion picture acting. | Personal coaching.
Classification: LCC PN1995.9.A26 D74 2018 | DDC 791.4302/8–dc23
LC record available at https://lccn.loc.gov/2018002428

ISBN: HB: 978-1-350-03942-1
          PB: 978-1-350-03943-8
          ePDF: 978-1-350-03941-4
          eBook: 978-1-350-03944-5

Typeset by Integra Software Services Pvt. Ltd.
Printed and bound in Great Britain

To find out more about our authors and books visit www.bloomsbury.com and sign up for
our newsletters.

CONTENTS

25 **Wrapping It Up** 142

ACKNOWLEDGEMENTS

So many people have helped me arrive at a place where I have enough to write a book. The hundreds of actors, directors and teachers I have worked with. My mentors and coaches. My friends and family.

So, here we go with a severely shortened list.

Firstly, my children Kayleigh and Matthew, who have reinforced in me the depths of the human imagination and the commitment to a story. My wife, Catherine, for her unending support and discipline. My mother and father for giving me the tools to set out on the journey in the first place.

My coach Jill McCulloch, who got me off my butt. Marcilie Smith Boyle, who kept me off it. My acting coaches George Loros, Robert Castle and the staff at The Lee Strasberg Theater Institute in New York City. The staff at the Actors Centre in London past and present, particularly Louise Cole and Michael John who told me to write the book in the first place. Michael Ferguson, whose encouragement and brilliance started me off on the road to teaching, coaching and setting it down on paper and his co-conspirator in his journey into the mind of the actor, renowned hypnotherapist Robert Lewis. The Actors Screen Collective alongside whom this expedition was experienced. The trainers from The Coaches Training Institute who gave me tools to help others. The actors of the London Screen Project in my Monday class, who helped me hone my ideas; Jane Paul-Gets, Robin Morrissey, Victoria Morrison and Andy Coxon, whose sterling work is seen in the online video exercise clips. And the hundreds of actors I have had the pleasure of working with over the last twenty-plus years.

And, of course, my publishers, Lucy, Anna, John and Camilla at Bloomsbury/ Methuen Drama, without whom this would only be an idea and not reality. Thanks!

INTRODUCTION

Working in the entertainment industry for over twenty years as an actor, director, teacher and coach, I have been struck by the myths and complexities promoted by those who state how *difficult* acting is rather than how *simple*. I have noticed how attitude directly impacts performance and characterization, how state of mind makes line learning easier or harder, how actors' concerns about the way they look or where their next job will come from reduces their ability to live the life of the characters they are employed to play. Because, after all, that is what acting is about: putting yourself in the mind, body and soul of another human being. If you are reading this book I'm assuming you are the kind of actor who wants to live and breathe your characters, feel what they feel and pass their humanity on to the viewer.

The phrase *acting from the inside out* is well known but the combination of life-coaching and acting technique provides an additional level – acting from *inside* the inside out, providing a solid, uncluttered and clear foundation upon which to build your characters and roles. Once you move away from your own limitations and obstacles and establish greater simplicity, control, confidence and self-knowledge there will be more space to employ specific acting techniques and focus on your characters and *their* hopes, dreams and obstacles. Basically, getting out of your own way before getting into the lives of others.

Life-coaching is a focused, specific and positive exploration into the lives of those who want clarity, direction, fulfilment and the most out of life. In layman's terms, it means that you identify, keep and develop the good stuff and target and remove the bad. *A Life-Coaching Approach to Screen Acting* recognizes the build-up of *stuff* which stands in your way, dulls your performance and limits the character's chances for spontaneity and truth; and then helps you to remove it. *Stuff*, such as confidence and nerves, whether people will like and employ you again, have you *perfected* your role, reached the *right* emotional level, and mastered all the technical considerations.

Clearing space and experiencing the resulting freedom will allow you to relieve pressure, manipulate your brain and focus your mind on the character's thoughts, behaviours and emotions. You will be free to paint on a blank canvas for the benefit of your craft and your audience, as well as truly enjoy the career you have chosen. You will take the *stuff* and put it all in a sound and smell-proofed box to be consciously opened only when you need to use it to help inform your roles.

A central tenet of coaching is that you, the client, know all your answers and already have everything you need inside you. You are capable of understanding and feeling everything and, as Freud declares many times, you may already have done so in your very early lives. You already know how to love, hate to the point of murder, belittle, challenge and so forth. Some Buddhist teaching claims that we are born knowing everything and spend our lives trying to remember it. The point is that once you believe in and trust yourself and remove your own obstacles, you will be able to creatively and freely access the entire range of emotions, characteristics, truths and journeys of the characters you are asked to play.

By better knowing yourself you will learn to separate your thoughts as an actor from those of your character and concentrate on who *they* are and what *they* want. You will replace perfectionism and overcritical self-analysis with focused hard work and the notions of being satisfied with working *towards* something and of being *as good as you can possibly be. Success* becomes understandable, tangible and achievable, and getting out of your own way and freeing yourself from personal obstacles will result in exciting, real, believable and colourful acting.

A Life-Coaching Approach to Screen Acting is divided into four parts:

Part One – *What is holding you back?* This uses life-coaching techniques and practical exercises to clearly establish who you are and who you are not. It helps identify what is holding you back so that you may move forward and freely work on and embody the characters you play.

Part Two – *Moving forwards.* This explores confidence, success and trust in yourself and your work. It identifies how learning occurs and how you can own and enjoy your progress.

Part Three – *As you are moving towards someone else* explores essential elements of your craft, such as emotions, imagination, nerves, focus, listening and line learning.

Part Four – *Tools to live someone else's life* offers practical thoughts and tools to then create powerful, real and believable characters and performance.

You will need a notebook and pen, or a couple of fingers to type into your tablet, and it will help if you have a video camera or camera phone and a tripod or selfie stick. Practical exercises, some of which are backed up by links to video files of hands-on coaching sessions enhance the learning. Audio files of guided meditations will take you on a mental journey to meet yourself and the characters you work on and deepen your understanding of both.

The focus is on you as a screen actor, but it will also benefit your stage acting.

Let me add a word of caution. Any teacher who demands a strict adherence to their style is not doing you a service. Acting is not a science. Take from this book what you want and leave the rest by the wayside. You will agree with much of what I say (hopefully) but I doubt if you will buy into it *all*; just as not all *Meisner* or *Method*, or *anything*, is *all* right for you.

Consider what you want to get from reading this. Challenge yourself and set your own personal goals and targets to help you on your journey. Write them down and check how far you have come at the end.

And, most of all, enjoy it!

PART ONE

WHAT IS HOLDING YOU BACK?

1
GET OUT OF YOUR OWN WAY

Before you can freely get into the mind, body and soul of other human beings – the characters you play – you must first recognize, acknowledge and remove your own personal obstacles.

When you were born, you were free of inhibitions and encumbrances. You screamed, smiled and slobbered at will and as you started to talk and walk you became an actor, using your imagination to soar to heights and sit on clouds or morph into a shark and swim to the bottom of the deepest oceans. You walked on molten lava and spoke with imaginary friends in your imaginary palaces. You accumulated behaviours and experiences and played with them. You mimicked those around you performing your version of their image, taking on the traits of your parents who helped you pronounce mummy and daddy in the dialect of their choice.

You grew to love the roar of the audience, the heartbreak of loss (when another child took your Thomas the Tank Engine), and the deep bonds and nature of true love. You learnt to lie when it suited you and regret telling the truth when it didn't.

Your imagination worked as a soliloquy, a monologue or as dialogue with a larger and varied cast, made up of loved ones, hated ones, unknown ones and imaginary ones.

Due to this early education, all the necessary skills to become a committed, powerful, colourful, real and believable actor are there inside you, as they have been since you were born. Your job is merely to get out of your own way, be true to your basic instincts and allow access to, and use of, what you already know. With the addition of learning lines and some technique of course, but you get the point.

But what do I mean when I say *get out of your own way* and why is it so important?

Getting out of your own way means removing or ignoring old experiences, habits, behaviours, thoughts, anxieties and doubts which may prevent you from fulfilling the task in hand – which in this case, is acting. Once these burdens stop being liabilities you can accept and consciously employ them when your character necessitates, then switch them off again when you leave the set.

At whatever age you are reading this, life has already layered on an extra amount of *stuff* to who you are. Exterior and interior restrictions and inhibitions have been built up and layered on like silt on a river bed. This comes from your parents, family, school, everyone you've ever met and everything you've seen, heard and done.

You have been told to lower your voice, speak up, not to cry or laugh too loudly, to not feel or display emotions, to be sensible and not daydream, to not exaggerate, keep a stiff upper lip, always ask permission and don't start a venture until you are certain you will succeed rather than trusting yourself and working on instinct. You have been told to accept that things are the way they have always been, that denial is okay, not to question authority and always respect your elders.

Imagine your life's journey as one of those long, straight, dry roads cutting through the heart of America or Australia. You know the ones, with a mountain range off in the distance and dirt tracks leading to nowhere. You can clearly see through your windscreen where you are going and, in your rear-view mirror, where you came from. The terrain is beautiful and you drive, at the speed limit, with the top down, the smell of nature in your nostrils and the warmth of the sun against your skin.

But imagine you are travelling down this road and littered in front of you are all the barriers and blocks which you have accumulated in your life thus far and you can't see the road ahead clearly enough to drive at a sufficient pace. You must weave in and out of these obstructions and take a circuitous route, sometimes moving backwards before you can move forwards.

At the other end of the road is where you want to get to, but you can't until you've cleared the way. Any fixes are like sticking plasters and you clear one rock only to encounter a similar one further along. Gravel and stones jump up and crack your windscreen and make pock marks in your bodywork which accumulate and become rusty and difficult to repair.

Clearing the rubble is what I mean by *getting out of your own way*. Cleaning the road of the rocks, soda cans, junk and clutter, choosing to stay on the main road and stop off in a town on the way for a leisurely lunch, rather than being forced to make unwanted detours which slow or stop your journey. It's a rhetorical question but wouldn't you find it preferable and more enjoyable to clean up the debris and drive more freely for longer?

Grotowski's concept of the *Via Negativa* (Grotowski, 1975) refers to acting truthfully as *not a collection of skills but an eradication of blocks*, eliminating the obstacles which are blocking your creative expression, ability and spontaneity. Actors in their own way possess an extra layer of their own *stuff* between what they are performing and what the audience receives. It is akin to climbing a mountain with a backpack full of rocks. There are so many rocks that there is no space for anything else and as you drag yourself up, the heavier it gets and the less opportunity there is for progress.

Getting out of your way allows you the freedom to creatively, unselfconsciously and straightforwardly access parts which have been covered up. After your homework and research is done, you will trust it and put it aside, act and react in the moment and be free to laugh, cry or shout. You will free yourself from the need to plan everything in advance and deliver your lines in the same way every time, and avoid an intellectual performance devoid of life and humanity. Seeing instead the human inside/behind and understanding what makes them tick.

How can you channel the character's emotional range if you cannot freely manage your own? Getting out of your own way is like pulling back a curtain to expose a huge canvas upon which you can paint whatever is required, using your own skills, in your own style and with your own imagination. You can paint from a broader palette, access deeper places, trying fresh, diverse ways of doing things, creating new experiences rather than merely reacting through your past conditioning.

Grotowski says you can support this via a *complete stripping down … laying bare one's own intimacy*, to *achieve a freedom from the time-lapse between inner impulse and outer reaction*, so that *impulse and action are concurrent*.

Actors must reveal themselves and be able to control when not to reveal themselves. Societal build-up has prevented many of us from being willing or able to do this. We don't want people to see us as sad, overconfident or angry, so we deny that we are feeling it. This denial is heaped upon us like the silt in the river which eventually blocks the flow and creates stagnant pools where once a free-flowing force of nature existed.

People watch television or go to the cinema to be affected. They want to laugh and cry and feel something they cannot during their daily lives. They need to feel what you feel, but they can only do so if you feel it yourself.

Your chosen profession can be nerve-wracking, unfulfilling and sparse if you let it but it should be fun and give you satisfaction and fulfilment. The great Paul Newman (IMDB, n.d.) said that *to be an actor you have to be a child*, and I agree. Enjoy the work and life, grab it with both hands and embrace it. If you get out of your own way and allow life to flow, it will, more than likely, give you fulfilment, joy, a career and financial reward.

One of my clients recently commented that they were so happy to get back in touch with how they were as a 7-year-old when they served imaginary food from their imaginary café. And as I watch my 7- and 8-year-old kids unabashedly and truthfully work the same café, I can see how the rules and regulations they will face will close off many of their creative, imaginative and entertaining parts.

I'm suggesting that you take this back. Reawaken your inner child. Get paid to be that 7-year-old walking on lava and serving cappuccinos. Have that *joie de vivre* (joy of life!) and reflect upon it from an adult perspective with all your learnt knowledge and safety.

I'm not suggesting that you behave like a sociopath with no control over yourself, nor that you constantly express emotions or are rude to people on the street. Life is not one big open road down which you can drive how you want and as fast as you want. There are rules which exist for good reason. Not all roads are straight and clear, and weaving along at 120 miles an hour on a winding crowded one may not turn out well. I am assuming that you know the basic difference between right and wrong and fight and flight. Many of the imposed *do's* and *don'ts* highlighted above are necessary in society and, with relevance to your chosen career, on a set. Knowing to look both ways before crossing the road prevents you from getting run over and taking care not to stick your finger in the power generator avoids you getting fried/fired.

There is a time and a place for everything and the beauty of being an actor is that you have plenty of times and places where you can shout at people, have one-night stands, and love and hate in equal measure. Then at the end of the day, switch it all off.

A cautionary note on creativity: whilst fear of failure, a sense of inadequacy and all the other pressures will not help you, be wary of removing *all* the stuff you have accumulated. It is this which gives you your character and personality and makes you an artist. What is important is to access, use and make sense of it rather than be limited and dictated to by it. *Stuff* is the raw material. Growing up with negativity, hardship and restriction can be useful if you are able to employ it to play a specific role in a specific script. If the character has had their self-belief squashed by circumstances and you can truly relate to and access that, you will not have to reinvent the wheel to live it.

If you are at an audition worrying about *stuff* such as getting it *right* or how your career will end up, you probably won't get the part. Bryan Cranston wisely stated that:

> the best advice for fellow actors is this: know what your job is ... An actor is supposed to create a compelling and interesting character that serves the text. You present it in the environment where your audition happens, and then you walk away. And that's it. Everything else is out of your control, so don't even think of that, don't focus on that, you're not going there to get a job, you go there to present what you do, you act. And there's power in that, there's confidence in that. (Bryan Cranston's Advice to Aspiring Actors, 2013)

The biggest obstacle to you moving forward is generally yourself. It's not so much about learning new skills but more about freely accessing existing ones. In real life, you've met most of the characters you will play or have at least read about them or seen them on TV. Your mind and body know exactly what to do, so just get out of your way and let them do it.

2
VALUES AND FULFILMENT

You are the sum of your parts. Identifying, clarifying and strengthening them will make you a stronger actor as well as clearer and more confident as a person.

The seven sages of ancient Greece who laid the foundation for Western culture at the Temple of Apollo carved *know thyself* on the entrance to the courtyard of the sacred oracle in Delphi. The French poet George Sand later went on to ask *can one know oneself*? I believe that the answer to this is, yes, you can.

But why does it matter for you as an actor and how can you achieve it?

True self-knowledge and acceptance of who you are can bring control and confidence on numerous levels, including as a person, in your craft and in your career. It can help pinpoint the roles you play and the medium in which you want to play them and provide a foundation upon which to shape a fulfilling and successful career. If you know you play fragile girls next door, or jokers with an edge, or total bastards, you can forge a career based on this knowledge, while saving yourself time and money by focusing your energy and resources towards it. If you are not a leading lady/man you must not promote yourself as if you were one. If you are quirky, see yourself as such. If you are a nerd, accept it. When you accept who you are and promote yourself as such, the casting people will also have a clearer picture and will be more confident bringing you in.

By identifying and accepting who you are the business side of *show business* becomes more natural and you can maintain your integrity when engaging with it. The work becomes about the work itself not about impressing people or dreaming of the Hollywood sign in the middle of a take. More on this later.

An exploration and understanding of yourself and what makes you unique as a human being starts with your values, which influence your personality, motivations and experiences.

You are made up of your values. They are what makes you tick and are the foundation stones upon which you stand. When fully present they create resonance and fulfilment, but when they are absent or are being insufficiently honoured, generate dissonance, frustration and stagnation.

Once you identify these elements which make you *you*, you can change your life for the better, make healthier choices, identify what is and isn't important and act in ways which improve you, rather than hold you back. Values drive attitude and intention and through them you pinpoint the component parts which influence your decisions and actions.

To one degree or another, values are present in everything you do. Writing this book is playing to my values of sharing knowledge, helping others be all they can be and making an impact.

You may have been told what your values are by other people including your parents, teachers and friends but you will benefit from deciding them for yourself. Choose your life based on who you are, not on how society has instructed you to be.

Your values may include integrity, honesty, creativity, independence, friendship, family, identity, connection, community, hard work, reciprocity, respect, justice, generosity, fairness and so on and so forth.

What is important is not having the value itself but living that value to its fullest and maximizing its impact. Being virtuous is better than wanting to be virtuous. Living a life full of humour and fun will provide more resonance than simply noticing that it is important for you.

'Know thyself' was written over the portal of the antique world, said Oscar Wilde. *Over the portal of the New World, 'Be Thyself' shall be written* (Wilde, 1891).

When the majority of your values are resonating concurrently you will be free and prepared to do anything you want. You will build a stronger momentum and put a greater energy into your parts and projects. Honouring your values will help you choose projects more carefully and decide upon their moral or creative merits. If you are constantly being offered terrorist roles and it makes you feel uncomfortable then tell your agent not to put you up for them. For some, playing Adolf Hitler may be a challenging role of a lifetime but it may cause others to hate themselves.

It is important to recognize that your values may change as you get older. What was necessary at high school may not be so when you are in your thirties, forties or seventies. Coming out of drama school at 21 with a strong community value may not be as important later in life as if you leave at 60. Or vice versa.

If you clearly know yourself you will have an obstacle-free playing field upon which to play, making it easier to effectively relate to and identify with the strengths and weaknesses of your characters. Once you have a clear knowledge of your principles you can look at the characters you play and assess what makes *them* tick; the similarities will be clear and you can determine and work on those characteristics which you don't possess. For example, playing Napoleon, Cleopatra or Norman Bates, you may readily associate with some of their inner life – such as their deep love, overwhelming sense of duty or fierce independence – then identify and add any which you don't instantly relate to, such as need for control and dominance over others or willingness to use extreme violence to get what you want.

Identify your values

EXERCISE

You can identify your values by looking at your life and analysing what is important for you. Pull potential values out from the following questions and list them:

- Think of two people you admire most and consider what you particularly respect about them; e.g. is it integrity, dedication, hard work, social awareness, generosity?
- Ask yourself what brings joy and inspiration into your life, e.g. creativity, variety, family and friends.
- What motivates you? Is it recognition, achievement, fun and enjoyment?
- Think about times when you have been at your most resonant and complete and look at the reasons why in relation to potential values. If it was in a show, what was it about the experience? Fitness, connection, relaying of powerful messages?
- Look for decisions you have made, think about how much your values were honoured or ignored and how you felt as a result.

Click on this link for a sample values clarification session and extend your list further – https://vimeo.com/251793351.

Once you have drawn up a list, figure out your top ten and put them in ranking order in the values table in Appendix 1. Prioritizing them will make you think harder about what they mean and how much they mean to you. I have added a sample completed table in Appendix 2 to help you further.

It is important to clearly and cleanly clarify your values and not lump them all into a catch-all word. For example, hard work/drive/determination may have separate energies and separating them may give you a broader self-knowledge. You may be hard-working but willing to spend your career playing bit parts to spend more time with your family rather than on sets.

Keep going deeper into what each value means to you. Travel may feel like a value but what does travel bring to you that is so essential? Is it adventure, variety, peace, newness? You may even come up with values that don't make sense to anyone else, such as fizzling butterfly or effervescent pragmatist.

When filling in the second column in the table recognize that it is not important for anyone else to know what you mean by the value as long as you do.

A word of warning: don't pick values because you think other people will be impressed if you say you have them. Don't write *honesty* if you don't really *need* to be honest. Be honest with your list.

The next column asks for a score between 1 and 10 with 1 being not at all honouring and 10 being totally doing so.

Once you have a number, come up with one thing you can do to increase this score by one point. For example, creativity may be a value but you are only at a 5 because you are working as an understudy and never get on stage. There is a lot of hanging around in the dressing room and time just flies, so at the end of every day you feel dissonant as nothing has been achieved. To increase your score, you could download a script with a character you would like to play, read the script, work on the backstory of the character and learn their lines. It may also feed into other values such as personal development or work.

EXERCISE

Do the above exercise to deepen your understanding of a character you are working on or one from the TV drama *Friends and Crocodiles* by Stephen Poliakoff (Poliakoff, 2005) which we will be using later in the book. Choose ten resonant values and create a backstory and motivations around them. For example, if you decide that one of your characters has a deeply held value of honesty, consider what this means for them in detail. Give them a low current score out of 10 and consider how this is impacting on their day-to-day life, then contemplate how they can increase the score.

Fulfilment

I have been using the word *fulfilment*, but what do I mean? A description may be *a state of contentment, certainty and firing on all cylinders; the completion and achievement of desires, needs and wants*. Or, more simply, that feeling when you are on top of the world and anything/everything is possible.

There are many reasons why it is important for you, as an actor, to be fulfilled. Let's take the audition scenario as an example. You may be the best actor in the world but if you walk into the audition room feeling sorry for yourself, miserable, needy, bitter and negative then the likelihood of you getting the job must be lower than if you were feeling the opposite. If they are looking for someone to work with a small crew in a remote location for a month they will not want to hire a misery guts. If they have a choice between an actor who is not quite as good as you but nicer to be with, they will choose that person and edit around them. A negative influence on any team, especially a tightknit cast and crew, could very well destroy the project. There are many examples of big projects which have gone wrong for this reason.

Also, our industry can be unforgiving if you let it get to you. If you are depressed going in and out of every audition, the number of auditions will decrease, feeding back into the negative cycle, until they stop bringing you in, thus confirming your negative view.

The wheel of life

Values are an important component of fulfilment, but they don't make up the total picture as different areas of your life need different considerations.

EXERCISE

Using the wheel of life in Appendix 3, divide your life into career, money, health, friends and family, relationships, personal development, fun and recreation, home and personal environment.

Using the key, allocate a score between 1 and 10 for each of these sections and see how fulfilled you are. The next step, as before, is to incrementally increase your scores. If personal development, for example, is a 3/10, look for a way to increase the score, connecting the actions to the types of parts you want to play. If you want to be in *Game of Thrones* or play sword and sandals roles, learning how to ride a horse or wield a sword will both aid your personal development and make you more marketable as an actor.

If career has a low score, break it down into smaller parts and incrementally increase those individual scores over time. Itemize agents, casting directors, special skills, on-camera training, accents, stage combat and so on, and do one extra positive action for each. You will find that the sum of these smaller parts will powerfully strengthen the whole (see the later section on Marginal Gains).

3

SABOTEURS AND LIMITING BELIEFS

You have a choice; listen to your gremlins, negative chatter and limitations, or focus on the part of you which has self-belief and positivity.

Humans are complex animals whose attitudes can be consciously and unconsciously changed from positive to negative and vice versa at the drop of a hat. We can be friendly, happy and fun then unfriendly, miserable and mean. Some people like being miserable and are comfortable living with self-doubt and low self-esteem whereas others glide through life on a cloud of positive energy.

It is said that *misery loves company*, and that *the only thing more contagious than enthusiasm is a lack of enthusiasm*. But who wants to be with someone with a negative energy for a protracted period? Not casting directors or film crews, I can assure you. And what about inside your own head? Would you rather be happy or sad? Active or passive? Confident or not? Is it easier to carry out a task with a positive frame of mind or a negative one? I would say that the former will serve you in better stead than the latter and replacing a negative attitude with a more positive one will help you get more work and enable you to do a better job when you get it.

Many of us have a saboteur who sits firmly on the negative side of this equation, attempting to undermine our plans and efforts and sabotage our progress. Your saboteur sounds rational, logical and mainly unthreatening and seems to have your best interests at heart. But don't be fooled, their job is to keep you in the same place and prevent you from moving forward.

Your saboteur, inner critic or gremlin has been a powerful and influential voice in your head since you were born, telling you who you are and what your place is in the world, and it is easy to not notice they are around. They stop you from being too creative, too active, too loving and too, pretty much, everything else. They draw on previous *failures* to prove their point, and will make you fail to prove that you are a failure; so you can securely live in this failure comfort zone. This has become what you know and you feel safe here. It generally exists in your head as opposed to your heart or gut and for some it is stronger than for others. Your saboteur can be dominant, assertive, definite and clear.

Below is a list of saboteur statements which you may recognize and be able to add to. They are comments which can pop up at any time, whether to reassure you that mediocrity and stasis are perfectly reasonable places to be, or that it is *unrealistic* to expect more than you have or are able to get.

Saboteur words and phrases

- It's not realistic.
- I'll never be able to do that.
- I'm not good enough.
- There are a thousand people up for the role, I'll never get it.
- I am comfortable with the saboteur voice as it's a boot up the ass.
- I'm not good at networking/marketing/creativity, etc.
- I am not enough.
- I haven't got enough.
- I will never have enough.
- I don't deserve it (see chapter on The Impostor Syndrome).

Saboteurs can manifest themselves in many forms; as male, female, animal, mineral, vegetable, a ball of dust, someone famous or your piano teacher from school. Your first instinct may be to fight them – to try and chop their head off – but this is unwise. If you think you have gained a final victory, only for it to rear its ugly head again, you will have *failed* and your saboteur will win.

But fear not, the saboteur is not all powerful and you can move beyond its negative influence by using the following three steps:

1) The first step is to recognize that you have one.
2) Then notice how often they speak to you, their self-limiting statements, and how comfortable you are with them.
3) Then ignore, dismiss or laugh at them and focus on something else.

Over 2,500 years ago, the ancient Chinese philosopher and writer Lao Tzu stated that one should *simply notice the natural order of things. Work with it rather than against it. For to try to change what is, only sets up resistance.* Basically, if you try to fight it you bring attention to it and this is what gives it power, like a naughty schoolboy. The age-old statement of *ignore him and he'll go away* comes to mind.

To deal with your saboteur, define what they look, sound, smell, taste, and feel like and be clear about who/what it is. Personify or give them a shape or embodiment so you know what you are ignoring. Then mentally or physically do something practical to remove them.

Some examples:

- One of my clients uses her ex-husband as her saboteur and puts him in the wet room (of her imagination) which he had installed against her wishes a short while before they divorced.

- Another was on a reality TV show where an unfairly critical judge berated and belittled her in front of millions of viewers. This debilitated and prevented her from moving forward in her career, believing she was a rubbish actress who would never progress. Once she recognized that she had a saboteur, she named it after this judge – who will remain nameless – mentally put them in a garbage truck which was driving past at the time of our conversation, and watched it drive off. Now every time she notices her negative chatter she mentally puts her gremlin in the garbage truck and sends it on its way.

- Another client had his gremlin sitting on his shoulder like the devil in the *Animal House* movie. Now, every time he hears its voice he brushes it off with his hand and is now a regular on a highly respected TV series.

- One of my personal gremlins is the cartoon character Droopy who always seems to want to not do things. Dealing with Droopy has not been easy whilst writing this book, but I did not let him win. I printed out an image and put it on my wall as a warning.

EXERCISE

Identifying your saboteur:

- Hear, visualize and personify them – maybe it's a person who has dragged you down or made you feel inadequate. Maybe it looks like one of the Gremlins from the movie of the same name, or your drama teacher, or an amalgamation of many people or things. Maybe they have a nasal whining voice or a booming roar. Find an image to print out or have in your mind to make them specific, thus making it easier to manage.

- Give them a name.
- Imagine a place to put them, such as a box with a lid; or an action to dismiss them, such as a gentle sweep of your hand or a blink of an eye; or when they appear, gently or assertively tell them that you don't wish to speak to them. See what works for you; there is no right or wrong.
- Write down your negative saboteur statements then throw away the paper.

- And practise, of course.

Limiting beliefs

Beliefs are powerful. They are formed through repeated ideas or actions which you then hold as being true. They dictate what and how you think and what you do with those thoughts.

Beliefs become limiting if they stop you believing in yourself or moving forward with a project or even life itself.

You may have experienced or used some of the following in your career so far:

- the same people get all the roles
- I didn't go to the right drama school
- my accent is not 100 per cent
- hard work has to be hard
- once you're an adult, life is about responsibilities, not fun
- I don't have time
- dreams are not practical
- I don't know what I'm doing
- my voice is boring
- I look boring
- I am boring

Most beliefs are formed unconsciously without our knowing and we would probably not have accepted the negative ones if we had known how it would end up. If the saboteur had not been hanging around feeding on them, they may even have passed on through and not become beliefs at all. Unless you are a masochist, you wouldn't actively seek out or repeat thoughts which become conclusions that keep you from experiencing the life you want. Right?

But that is what you do; after which you cement, fasten and keep it as law until it becomes the way it has always been. Until you get older, by which time you believe that you are too old to change. Supposedly.

The longer the beliefs have been around, the more difficult they may be to notice and trickier to remove. You may have become so comfortable with them that you even feel a part of you is missing when they are gone.

The remedy, as with the saboteur, is not easy but relatively straightforward, and it takes will power. Recognize the need to change, then commit to doing something about it. It is changeable no matter how much you think it isn't. Take action and live the change, push your boundaries, stretch your comfort zone and break patterns. Apathy may be a major obstacle and strong if you allow it.

EXERCISE

- Question your saboteur's logic with an objective view and think outside yourself as if you were counselling a good friend over the same issue; e.g. who said I'm not good at accents? Was it just one person when I was 8 years old or one of my teachers at drama school? Surely developing accents is trainable? Where is the evidence that I can't do it? According to which scientific scale? Have I made an effort to practise one sentence at a time or in bite-sized chunks, i.e. given myself a fair chance? Have I given it enough time to maximize my chances?
- Write down the internal commentary in your notebook then read it out aloud and recognize how ridiculously limiting it is.
- If you don't like the sound of your own voice, record and listen to yourself over and over until you accept how you sound. Normalize it.
- The same with how you look. Film yourself over and over and play it back. Get used to it. Once you do, self-taping will become quicker, easier and less stressful.

A note on your inner critic

The *Cambridge Dictionary* gives the definition of a critic as *someone who says that they do not approve of someone or something*. But why would you allow yourself to welcome a voice which does not approve of you? *Inner critic* is a phrase often used in a positive context and as a way of driving people forwards. Many of them claim that *I must listen to my inner critic* and *it's good to have an inner critic.* But why if it is so negative? The opposite of this self-approbation accompanying you into the audition room or onto the set will surely benefit you more? Acceptance of being who you are and being as prepared as you can be in the time you have had available will help, denigrating yourself will not.

Words obviously have an impact, so use ones which have a discernible benefit rather than the potential to hold you back. Listen to your positive self and call your saboteur and inner critic what they are; negative forces to be ignored. I will be introducing you to your *Captain* who will help you with this task, later in the chapter, but in the meantime, let's look at ...

Use of language

Will rather than *try*

- The word *will* is a powerful and decisive word. It means that you are going to do something rather than think about doing it, or hedge your bets that you may or may not do it.

- *try to* – *trying* to do something implies less than total effort or commitment. I will *try* to read the script before midnight tonight is not as powerful as I *will* read the script before midnight tonight. *Trying* to do something makes it potentially okay to not do it.

- You cannot *try* to concentrate because the trying part is what takes you out of the undertaking. If you are thinking about concentrating then you are not doing it.

- *Trying* to do something implies that you don't trust yourself enough to just do it and get it done. As the Nike slogan says, *Just do it!*

- *Trying* to be attractive and interesting to others is hard to sustain as casting directors – like potential life partners – smell desperation and insecurity a mile away. Self-confident people don't need to try, they just do.

Give it a go

With the same logic, saying *I will give it a go* is not the strongest entry point into a venture. *Giving it a go* implies a tentative dip of your toe into the pool with a pre-ordained acceptance of potential non-committal or non-action.

Should

Saying *should* is equally a cop-out. Avoid the *should be syndrome* – *should be* reading scripts instead of reading scripts, *should be* learning an accent rather than *will be*. *Should* serves as a pipe dream or something you would like to do but are not willing to commit to.

Want to

Ditto!

I statements

Feel the difference in energy when you change

you walk into a room and everyone is looking at you. You do your monologue, leave, and you think that was terrible,

to

I walked into the room and everyone was looking at me. I did my monologue, left, and it was terrible.

Or

you are insecure about auditioning and you don't get as many parts as you want,

as opposed to

I am insecure about auditioning and I am not getting as many parts as I want.

Or

it hits you hard in the heart and you can't stop crying,

as opposed to

it hits me hard in my heart and I can't stop crying.

Using *I* instead of *you* when talking about yourself brings a sense of ownership and taking responsibility for what you think, say and do. You own the statement and its consequences. I have had many clients who become emotional once they make this change. They grasp that it is about them, not some removed other person.

Negative language

The brain cannot hold a negative as a negative and you may not achieve your desired intentions if you do not understand this. Wherever possible, use positive statements rather than negative ones. If I say *don't think of a yellow elephant*, what's the first thing you think about? Keep on not thinking of a yellow elephant. Go on, I dare you. So, when you say to yourself *I don't doubt myself,* your brain logs the *I doubt myself* part. Try changing to something like *I have confidence in my ability* (see later section on neuroplasticity).

Fear

Fear restricts creativity and as creativity is essential for a performer it prevents you from doing the best job that you can do. The saboteur feeds on fear: fear of failure and of success, fear of the unknown, of looking stupid, of inadequacy and powerlessness, fear of how you look and sound, of never being employed again. Will I make it or will it be all worth it? Fear of being found out that I'm not actually any good (see The Impostor Syndrome).

If you look at your fears, you can easily claim that they are cautionary and true. But as with your saboteur, they can prevent you from taking action or enjoying the actions you do take. Roosevelt said *there is nothing to fear but fear itself* and he was right. Unless it is truly life and death and a vicious man-eating lion is licking its lips and seeing you as lunch, what you are undertaking must be way down the importance spectrum. After all, what is the worst that can *really* happen?

As fear is part of your saboteur it can be dealt with using the same tools. Recognize it, ignore it, focus on something else and move on. Stick it in the box and throw it away. If you commit to your task at hand the saboteur has no time or space to begin to be afraid. Before a sky dive, the time can be filled with fear and dread, but the second you jump out the door it is replaced by exhilaration. Wouldn't it be more fulfilling to lead up to this exhilaration with excitement rather than fear?

Getting help from your captain

As there is a side of you which is sabotaging your progress, there is also a side which is inwardly strong, non-judgemental, authoritative, creative, courageous and which loves and supports you unconditionally.

The Coaches Training Institute, in *Co-Active Coaching* (Kimsey-House et al., 2011), calls this your *captain* and, as with the saboteur, they can manifest themselves as male, female, animal, mineral, vegetable, an energy field or anything else, however personal or obscure.

Your captain's role is to help you recognize what is right for you and act on it. When you encounter situations where your saboteur is holding you back and you need support, you can consciously choose a positive voice to listen to instead.

EXERCISE

Go to https://vimeo.com/251793473 for an online guided meditation to meet your captain (the text can be found in Appendix 4). Find a quiet place by yourself, listen to the recording and let me do the work. When you have finished the exercise, practise standing then walking as your captain and feel their power and energy within you. Notice your posture, your shoulders and back, how grounded you feel, whether your feet or head is dominant. Work on embodying and making them a conscious asset.

Practise by asking your captain questions and, staying more in your body and out of your head, allow them to answer. The questions can range from minor ones, like *should I get my hair cut tomorrow* to more significant ones such as, *should I continue my acting career,* or *should I change my agent?* Practise when times are good and bad, so they are readily accessible when needed.

4
THE IMPOSTOR SYNDROME

There is a syndrome which can challenge your chances of progress and success. It makes you think that you are a fraud and afraid you will be found out. Many of the greatest actors have felt and feared the same. Fear not, though, you can overcome it.

I first heard about the Impostor Syndrome on a transatlantic flight from New York to London in the first-class bar. I was being flown over for a gig and felt great, schmoozing and boozing at 30,000 feet. However, underneath my bravado and assumed status, I was experiencing a sense of unease that my co-boozers had more right to be there than me. I was afraid that they would find out that I was not really a first-class flier and that the acting job I was flying over for was not a Stephen Spielberg movie or *Downton Abbey*. I had felt this before when, as a high-flier in the business world, I constantly strove for promotion so as never to stay in one place long enough to be exposed as ineffectual and overrated.

On taking my seat for landing, I relayed these thoughts to my director, who smiled in recognition and told me that I had a syndrome, the Impostor Syndrome. Excellent, I had never had a syndrome before!

She explained that many successful people had it and it was very common. A-list actors such as Meryl Streep, Emma Watson, Kate Winslet, Michelle Pfeiffer, Nicole Kidman, Don Cheadle and Matt Damon have talked about feeling like no-talent shams and frauds, not knowing how to act and living with a fear of being found out and fired.

I felt immediately safer and more confident. Firstly, I wasn't alone and what I was feeling was experienced by the most successful actors in the industry, and secondly, it was obviously manageable.

The idea of an Impostor Syndrome was originally presented in 1978 by clinical psychologists Dr Pauline Clance and Suzanne A. Imes, who studied the behaviours and attitudes of high-achieving women. They found that the vast majority of them believed, despite evidence to the contrary, that they would be discovered as frauds, that they did not deserve the success they had achieved, and that any success was purely luck, timing or a result of fooling others about their intelligence and competence.

Further research found that men also felt the same way; 70 per cent of all people feel like impostors or frauds at one time or another, and 40 per cent of successful people consider themselves so.

Falling short of ridiculously high expectations and the resultant anxiety and depression may ensure that even when you do well you are still unable to accept your accomplishments or achievements. On set, after your scene is completed, when the crew moves on to focus on the next shot and forgets that you exist, a vacuum is created where your saboteur can befriend your impostor. Or when your impostor doesn't allow you to enjoy the moment when people tell you that you're great and they loved your performance. All because you don't believe them. *What the hell do they know, I wasn't feeling it!* Of course, there are times when people say you were great to your face but rubbish you behind your back, but that is out of your control and not what I am talking about.

The need to work and push harder and faster – because if you slow down you will be found out – can lead to over-preparation, stressing about the detail, the search for unachievable perfection (see later chapter), and even burnout. As your confidence diminishes, you begin to tell people what you think they want to hear, rather than being true to your own creativity. And when praise comes you don't accept that it is based on ability, truth or reality.

If the Impostor Syndrome is not addressed, symptoms such as anxiety, stress, low self-confidence, depression, shame and self-doubt prevail. This is especially acute for actors who work preparing their roles alone for lengthy periods followed by very brief moments in the spotlight under intense scrutiny.

Every hiccup, hesitation or moment of uncertainty becomes amplified and can send you down a rabbit hole of insecurity. The Impostor Syndrome confirms extreme failure, inadequacy and what you see as justifiable negative feedback from others, limiting your ability to live in the moment as the character and explore their experiences.

Examples of impostor comments:

- I have no idea what I'm doing.
- I just got lucky.
- I shouldn't be here.
- I'm the least talented person in the room.
- Anyone can do it.
- It was nothing special.
- I'm not that smart.

- I'll never be able to do that.
- I can't do this.
- I'm going to get found out.

Many actors say that they are fine once they get on the set but they find auditioning tough. They feel exposed and judged with the panel seeing straight through them and their every failure, pimple and no-talent moment. To have a career in this industry of any magnitude, though, you have to come to terms with the fact that you must audition and that, during the process, people look at you before they give you a job.

What can you do about it?

The Impostor Syndrome is not recognized as a formal mental disorder and is curable without medication. Whether you feel comfortable with it or not, it is not your friend. Being so afraid of getting found out that you don't pursue your ambitions is a travesty and a waste of a life.

Fortunately, though, it lives in the same realm as the saboteur and the means of dealing with it are similar too. The first step is to notice and accept its existence and consequently normalize your feelings. Many actors who experience the Impostor Syndrome are unaware that others also have it, so discuss it with your colleagues, friends and family. It loses its energy once it has been exposed. Discussing it with the director on the plane relieved my pressure and allowed me to perform with a new-found and unattached freedom.

Once you have recognized its existence you can prove to yourself that this needless self-doubt is unfounded and start to own your successes rather than push them away. You are as intelligent, talented and capable as you think you are, not as others see you. Work hard, own your accomplishments and believe that you deserve to be here based on merit not on looks or the fact that you went to school with the casting director.

Question the logic. The casting director will not bring you in if they don't have faith in you and believe you can do the job. They have their own reputations on the line. You don't get cast because they feel sorry for you, to humour you, or that they'll wait till you get on the set to decide whether you can act. They cast you because they think you are right for the part and will do the job.

Instead of negatively comparing yourself to others just notice the differences and accept them. You are unique and have qualities which others do not possess. Focus on these qualities and accept your strengths.

Viewing your circumstances differently, otherwise known as *reframing*, is another useful tool in dealing with saboteurs and impostors, and we will explore this further later.

Also, focusing on what you are doing rather than what people think of you allows less space to the impostor. We will go more deeply into this in Part Four when we consider the *inner actor/character*.

Some quotes from people you may respect

As you have heard of most, if not all, of the following actors, they clearly didn't let their fears and insecurities hold them back. They pushed on through and filled the moments when their saboteurs and impostors were banished with enough creativity to be as great as we know them to be.

I don't know how to act anyway, so why am I doing this? – **Meryl Streep** (Smith, 2017)

Sometimes I wake up in the morning before going off to shoot, and I think, I can't do this; I'm a fraud; they are going to fire me – all these things. I'm fat; I'm ugly … – **Kate Winslet** (Obst, 2000)

I still think people will find out that I'm really not very talented. I'm really not very good. It's all been a big sham. – **Michelle Pfeiffer** (Shorten, 2013)

All I can see is everything I'm doing wrong that is a sham and a fraud. – **Don Cheadle** (Lee, 2004)

Any moment, someone's going to find out I'm a total fraud. – **Emma Watson** (Gevinson, 2013)

I would report to the set certain that this is the time you're going to be figured out. This is the time you're going to get fired, for sure. They are going to know this time. – **Renée Zellweger** (Johnson and Malkin, 2016)

You always feel like he's feeling: 'I don't deserve this'. – **Gwyneth Paltrow about Matt Damon** (Eby, 2009)

I just never know if I'm going to pull it off. I have terrible, grave concerns about my own ability. – **Matt Damon about himself** (Eby, 2009)

You can have a perfectly horrible day where you doubt your talent … Or that you're boring and they are going to find out that you don't know what you're doing. – **Meryl Streep** (AZQuotes, n.d.)

As a youth, I hated myself for not being good enough. All my inadequacies and failures, not being kind enough, generous or understanding enough, would assail me at night. It became a habit to be guilty and self-castigating, not liking myself because I was unworthy. There was no exit. I always had to be better, constantly never letting myself say 'Mira you're okay'. I really tortured myself. – **Mira Sorvino** (Dotson Rader, 1998)

EXERCISE

- Associate with your successes and strengths rather than fears and doubts. Make a list of fifty things you do well, big or small, whether whistling, accents, horse-riding or cooking.

- Then list fifty achievements you have made in the last two months, which can range from getting out of bed on time to being cast in a project.

- Read over these lists and notice how, when you leave your saboteur at the door, they aid what is commonly referred to as your *confidence*. Re-read your lists before you go into auditions, on the set or just for the hell of it.

- Listen out for impostor thoughts and comments and note them down. Then destroy the list if you wish.

5
PERFECTIONISM

Nothing in the universe is perfect. Strive to be driven and the best you can be. Plan your route and the tools you need. Enjoy the journey and make the destination more fruitful.

Perfect can be described as having no defects or flaws, and *perfectionism* is the need to regard anything short of *perfection* as intolerable. With a description such as this, why would you ever want to be a perfectionist? Perfectionism propagates the setting of unrealistic, severe and challenging goals where failure to achieve them is viewed as unacceptable and worthless. The belief that only 100 per cent will be good enough and you can't be satisfied with less can be self-destructive and restrictive, but many actors wear perfectionism as a badge of honour, believing it to be positive and essential in driving them forward.

Try to think of one thing in the entire universe that is perfect ... go on, anything ... truly perfect. It's not easy, is it? Everything has at least one flaw, even the most beautiful diamond or your favourite person or pet. Nothing is perfect but you expect to reach perfection yourself? This fixing of unreasonable, unattainable goals, and expecting to reach them, must be a sign of madness. By setting yourself up for disappointment and never being satisfied makes it impossible to enjoy the journey, as the destination, however elusive, is all that matters. You may touch upon perfection for a moment but this must be fleeting. For the long term, you can only find disenchantment and dissatisfaction.

As an actor, even for Daniel Day-Lewis, it is impossible to be *in it* – in your character and the action – 100 per cent of the time. If you do your preparation, of course, you will have lengthy periods when you are that person talking to the other person about something important, but then there are going to be times when you drop out. These are the moments when you can either beat yourself up or accept that life is not perfect, that stuff happens and maybe the editor will cut around that moment if it looks too wrong.

The irony of perfectionism is that it has the opposite impact than intended and actually creates inertia and lack of forward motion, rather than fulfilling drive. Perfectionists often believe that if you can't do it perfectly you won't do it at all, or give up at the first hurdle. You will never be as good as Meryl Streep or Robert De Niro, so why bother? You will never get an Oscar, so what's the point? Perfectionism does not perform as a driver, it acts as an obstacle which can never be overcome and consequently stops any drive at all. Your goal is to climb that huge mountain ahead and believe you will get there but it seems too daunting and huge to contemplate, let alone start.

I am *not* saying that you should merely be satisfied with what you have and stay where you are. But set yourself achievable targets and goals which stretch you, and enjoy the journey towards their realization.

An alternative approach is how to frame it. Break up your plan into bite-sized, manageable chunks each with an achievable goal. To climb the mountain, you must first make a plan, then go to the shop to buy boots, a tent, some pitons, a climbing axe, map and so forth. Then you hire a Sherpa/guide (or as an actor you would hire a coach) before you start out for base camp. After base camp, you go from stage to stage, raising your tent and resting by night and scaling the mountain inch by inch during the day. You avoid the falling rocks and ensure that you are working well in the team. You are always aware that the overall objective, or super objective, is to climb the mountain, but you are not focusing on the end result so rigidly that you neither manage the necessary stages, adapt to the unforeseen nor enjoy the journey.

Once you get to the top of the mountain you can stand there, enjoy the view and soak up the wonderful feeling of achievement. Then, from this state of achievement and satisfaction, look at the next range in front of you and decide if you want to repeat the process and how.

The same is true with your career as an actor. You must continue going to classes, learn skills, read scripts, practise vocal and camera technique, maintain a healthy body, audition, learn a role, finish the job and celebrate at the wrap party. Then look for more work and start all over again. Unless you enjoy this process, you should quit now. Being self-employed in any profession can be tough if you allow it to be, but if you have fun along the way, achieve your milestones and set new ones, you will be fulfilled enough to keep going. And if you get an Oscar along the way, all the better for you. Notice that I say *along the way*, not *in the end*.

So, how can you help relieve the pressure from yourself? As an actor, there is a totally understandable, acceptable and laudable need to be good or outstanding. However, I would like to introduce the concept of being good *enough*. It's like wanting to be the perfect parent, carpenter or footballer. It's impossible. You will make mistakes. You can only be good *enough*. The US Army advertising says, *Be all that you can be*, not *be perfect soldiers and people*.

Do all you can do in the time you have available, with the tools you have accessible and accept that. If you have a week to prepare for an audition you cannot bend time and make it two weeks. Will you ever have enough time? You are an artist who is studying the lives and times of others and as such you will never get to a finishing line of knowing everything there is to know. Make your own finishing line achievable. Learn *enough* and accept that it's enough to begin your performance. Thinking about *not* being ready or adequate will undoubtedly get in your way.

If you drop out the scene, don't panic. Relieve the pressure by grabbing hold of, and connecting with, one of the markers in the script which relate to what is going on with your character. Focus on something you have a solid image or opinion of. It may be your partner's face when you mention them dumping you for someone else, or buying salmon at the market if the line is about you promising to make dinner. It can be anything relevant. Then, like a mountain climber who uses an ice axe to pull themselves forward, use these markers to refocus and drag yourself back in and then progress through the scene. We will go into this further in Part Two but for now know that if there is no panic, moments of uncertainty and dropping out can become a part of the scene. And, once again, the editor can cut around you if it doesn't work.

When the audition/shot/scene/job is over, accept that what is done is done and what has passed is past. You cannot go back. It is the same for when things go well as when they don't. If you were really in the zone, felt it and satisfied with what you have done in the take, and go for an identical performance on the following take, you may disappoint yourself as it cannot be or feel exactly the same. You cannot repeat exactly the same performance and you shouldn't expect to.

If you have a solid technique and have done the prep work, it is enough to give a true performance. It doesn't help if you are judging whether what you did was good. Without controlling your expectations, you may spiral and disappear into self-consciousness, with the only means of return being to push, fake and make it worse. There are always slight differences in what you do from take to take, so accept and frame it as giving the director and editor more variety to choose from. If you can, sit in on an edit and see for yourself. Additionally, if the director asks you to do it in a number of different ways to give him this choice, it will not help if your style is to strive for the exact same performance every time.

Embrace your vulnerability and enjoy not being perfect. Be free to expose yourself. Reject the shame and fear where there is something you don't want people to see. Be worthy of making connections with others because this is what an actor does.

Have the compassion to be kind to yourself and others. Be your authentic self and not how you think others should see you. Being vulnerable is a *good* thing, it is necessary as it's what makes you special. As an actor, you must be willing and able to explore and create with the possibility that you may fail. If you do, then embrace that failure and move on to the next thing.

Striving for perfection negates this vulnerability and stifles your artistry as an actor. It hinders your ability to enjoy life and embrace uncertainty and causes you to blame others for your disappointments.

Brené Brown, a well-respected authority on vulnerability, states that *because I feel this vulnerable it means I'm alive* (Brown, n.d.). I am enough!

You are good *enough*, slim *enough*, clever *enough*; you are worthy of love, belonging and a career. Have a sense of courage. The word *courage* comes from the Latin word cor which means heart; so, tell the story of who you are with your whole heart and have the courage to be imperfect.

EXERCISE

- Study a picture of Mount Everest, close your eyes and gently breathe in and out. Once you have calmed the chatter in your head, open your eyes and observe the picture again. Look for a route to the top. Then close your eyes again and go through all you will need to do to get there. Envisage the planning and enactment of the plan and, when you reach the top, absorb the view, the sounds, the air and wind, the smells and tastes. Experience being there and remember all you had to do to get there. After you have basked in this feeling, for however long you want, find another mountain you would also like to climb and repeat the process.
- Now imagine your ideal career and go through the same process. Think through headshots, agents, castings, bookings, being called to the set, hearing it's a wrap, and going home after a job well done to find a new script in your letter box.
- Now imagine your ideal role and do the same. Envisage the call from your agent for the audition, the sides coming through, the research and line learning; then hair and make-up, your trailer, the crew and the words *cut, that's a wrap* at the end.

PART TWO

MOVING FORWARDS

6
CONFIDENCE, SUCCESS, PERSPECTIVE AND REFRAMING

Confidence cannot be bought or given, so gain it through your own endeavours. Define what success means for you.

Confidence

Confidence is a desirable and valuable asset in life but for an actor it is essential. When present, with so many people watching you work, you may produce your best and enjoy it; whereas when absent, it's a potential disaster.

But what *is* confidence and how can you get it?

Simply put, confidence is a strong belief in yourself and your powers or abilities. It is found through an accumulation of experiences, successes and failures and is truly synergistic; which, plainly speaking, means that the result is greater than the sum of the parts. Small incremental positive results build upon each other to form a solid foundation, upon which further successes then add to the momentum.

People talk about *getting* more confidence and *being* more confident and they often rely on others to give it to them. But the reality is that confidence is intangible. You can't buy it off the shelf, order it from Amazon or switch it on and off. Telling people to *be confident* is like saying *get over it* or *cheer up* and is much more easily said than done. Others cannot give it to you except for a fleeting moment. If you receive a pep talk from your director about how well they think you are doing, you may believe it until you get home, whereupon you conclude that they said it simply to keep you motivated. And thence your confidence is back to square one. Or, more likely, minus one.

Confidence must start with, and come, from yourself. Being concerned about other people's opinions of your worth is unhelpful as it is subjective and out of your control. You cannot live life trying to satisfy what you think other people want from you. How is that possible? How will you know *exactly* what they want? And what if there are two people in the same room who want two different things? People will either like what you are doing or they won't.

I was in a play a few years ago and on press night the twenty-four *critics* in the audience each gave a totally different write-up to what they had seen. Some thought I was magnificent whilst others (erroneously of course), thought I was not. If I had contorted myself to adapt to what they wrote, I would have gone mad and my performance would have been crippled.

Your saboteur, if you allow it to, will chip away no matter what *they* or *we* say. If we say you are brilliant but you think you are rubbish, it won't make any difference. You will brush it off as they're idiots, they don't know what they are talking about, I'm rubbish.

If you allow yourself to gain confidence through your own endeavours, however, you will become more self-sufficient and won't need the recognition of others. Reading a script in one sitting, doing an hour of voice work, getting a new agent, a small speaking part in a TV series, a lead role in a short film, your headshots done, your show reel edited, meeting a director at a networking event, working with a casting director in a workshop and so on and so forth, will all incrementally add to your confidence.

The absence of activity will have the opposite effect, of course, so the choice is yours.

The fact that there is competition should not impact your confidence either. You are not actually in competition with anyone else to get the job as they are doing their own thing and you are doing yours. The casting director does not want to waste their client's time by showing them ten similar people doing the same thing in the same way. You must be different and have different impulses otherwise the casting director would not have called you all in. They want to see what you bring and how you interpret the material. You may see the character as a happy-go-lucky guy who loves being on the wrong side of the law whilst the other guy sees him as a dark and devious loner.

Al Pacino was slated to play Han Solo in *Star Wars* and Matthew McConaughey and Macaulay Culkin were in competition with Leonardo DiCaprio for the lead in *Titanic*. Very different actors with very different experiences to bring. The competition was not based on them or their talents but on how they would fit in with the whole project. And you have no control over that.

A lot of actors don't enjoy what they do. They don't enjoy looking for work, getting the work, doing the work, or following up and getting paid for it. Don't be that person. Put aside the negatives and the hundreds of reasons why your saboteur says you can't do the job and you may find that confidence will appear like a genie out of a bottle.

But it ain't what you do, it's the way that you do it. Confidence isn't about shouting about how wonderful you are and how awesome everything is. You can be confident and at the same time respectful of the culture and society you live in. For example, the words *I am confident* are often seen as more acceptable in the United States than in the United Kingdom, the Brits being less likely to appear on their front foot tooting their own horns than their American cousins.

It's like the difference between being assertive and aggressive. Assertive people state their opinions, while still being respectful of others. Aggressive ones attack or ignore others' opinions in favour of their own.

EXERCISE

- Work for half an hour every day for two months on a new accent until you have mastered it.
- Then learn another for the next two months.
- Do the same with other skills such as yoga, sword fighting, singing.
- And so on – I'm sure you get the point.

Success

Confidence can be gained through an accumulation of successes, but what is success and what does it mean to you?

The initial answer to this question is usually money, status or recognition. However, it is worth scraping below the surface to get a handle on what this success specifically looks like. For example, it may be not about the money but what you can do with it. Do you become instantly more fulfilled and successful once the ticker crosses over $1 million from $999,999? If so, then how long will this feeling of success stay with you? The same is true for getting that big role you have always yearned for. If you don't get another job for two years afterwards do you still feel like a success?

The danger with success is that it is often a reflection of how other people see you. She is an Oscar winner therefore she is successful. He is a millionaire therefore successful. Success must be attached to your own personal fulfilment. Consider whether a poor but happy woman is more successful than a rich sad one.

Success is an ongoing, in-the-moment kind of thing. Yes, you will be successful reaching the summit of the mountain, being viewed by the world as at the top of your profession, but true success rests upon a foundation of more simple and tangible victories. Traversing an escarpment with limited oxygen, having successfully chosen the right equipment before you left, will last as long in your memory as the success of reaching the pinnacle.

And what happens if you put in maximum effort, enjoy the challenge but don't reach the summit? Are you *not* a success? What about the hundreds of hours of hard work, duty and engagement which went before? Do they count for nothing?

An Oscar is the most tangible and visible mark of success as an actor. You have been recognized by the industry and society as the best actor of that year. It, and you, cannot get any better. But how long can this success last? Will you be sitting in your Hollywood mansion like Norma Desmond clutching your successes in your hand while the rest of the world moves on?

Clearly, *successful* is an ongoing feeling and can be small as well as large. Tying your shoelaces when extremely drunk is a good example of one of life's smaller successes, as is getting a tax rebate or being invited to a casting director's Christmas party.

Success is related to your values. How fully are you living yours? If you live your life through your values then success becomes totally personal. You can use it as a positive motivator which drives you forward rather than an impersonal negative stick with which to beat yourself. It is what you get when you let go of what others want for you and own what you want and have for yourself. And take actions to get it.

How do you define yourself? If you had a billboard on the motorway about yourself what would it say? What would you want people to say at your testimonial party twenty years from now? *He won an Oscar so he was a successful actor. He didn't work for twelve years afterwards but he got a table in a lot of restaurants.* Or, *he was a successful actor because he worked constantly, had a full and contented family and social life and was a role model for all who met him*?

Success is purely a matter of perspective. If you will only feel successful once you have been awarded your Oscar, then you are potentially destined for an unsatisfying life. Success doesn't have to be a finishing line. If your perspective is that success includes your small victories along the way and that it breeds further success, then you are already successful and clearly more fulfilled.

To cement and build upon your successes you must celebrate them. If you do a great audition, wrap on a show or send out 100 introduction letters to casting directors, you must mark it and celebrate. Otherwise it becomes too general and loses much of its impact. Buy a speciality coffee or a pair of shoes you have always wanted and recognize that confidence is built from a series of definable achievements.

EXERCISE

Consider strongly and deeply what the word *success* means to you and write it in your notebook. If you believe that it is an Oscar then ask yourself what it is about winning an Oscar which makes it a success for you. The further you explore, the more you will uncover. You may find that it is about recognition, hard work or one of your other values, which makes the achievement of success attainable through other means as well as an Oscar. Don't stop striving for the Oscar but build it upon a foundation of smaller shorter-term successes.

Perspective

Your perspective is the way you see something. If you think that beer destroys lives, then from your perspective a bar is an evil place. But if you see beer as a societal lubricant then your perspective may be that it's a community hub.

If you are reading this book with little or no formal acting training, I wonder how much more confident you will feel if you know that neither Johnny Depp, Cameron Diaz, Brad Pitt nor Meg Ryan had acting lessons. If you have become more self-assured as a result, how come? What has really changed? The circumstances are the same and it's only your perspective which has altered.

The Latin root of the word perspective means *looking through*. If you look through life with the perspective that everything is hard, challenging and doomed to failure then that is what you will get. If you say, *that's just the way things are*, then that will be just the way things are and will ever be. Other options will not exist and the prophecy of inadequacy and stagnation will be self-fulfilling. If you limit your possibilities to what you have already encountered and what you believe is realistic then it will be very difficult to move forward.

The joy of perspective is that it is changeable and by changing your perspective on something you can change your whole approach to it. If someone insults you and you say to yourself *I'll take that as a compliment*, then the negative energy is removed. If you say, *I am already a successful actor and want to grow my career even further*, then you will feel more successful, more resonant and more forward thinking. And, unsurprisingly, other people will want to be around you and even offer you work.

Stop saying that acting is a difficult profession, the industry is tough and there is no work out there. Stop saying that the same people are getting all the work. These are not very helpful perspectives, and, in a short time, they can become beliefs.

Reframing

Reframing is a useful technique. Calling something by a different name can remove the negative energy and replace it with a more positive and valuable one. For example, change the words *I am a perfectionist* to *I will be all that I can be*. When Thomas Edison was trying to invent the light bulb, someone asked him how he could keep going after failing to make one over a thousand times. He told them, *I have not failed, I have successfully discovered 1,000 ways* not *to make a light bulb*. If the world gives you lemons make lemonade. Some may call it optimism, and why not?

As with changing your perspective, reframing is also an incredibly useful tool as it encourages you to look at the same thing in a different way. If you think that a script is rubbish you may instead see it as a puzzle to be unlocked. If your co-star says you can't act your way out of a paper bag, take it as a compliment and smile to yourself at the imagery. Basically, take the emotion out of it. A negative, frustrated and anxious attitude will not help and will more than likely stop you from free flowing and engaging with what you are supposed to be doing. Self-consciousness is the death of good acting.

I'm making this sound simple but, as with everything else, it takes a lot of practice.

EXERCISE

- Take any feature of your life with which you feel blocked and write it on a piece of paper. It may be having to move to the suburbs, a stagnating career or an unhappy relationship. Put the paper on the floor in front of you and study it deeply, considering your current perspective and what you think about every aspect and emotion in relation to it, e.g. having to travel longer distances to get to auditions, fewer networking opportunities, lessened personal development, curtailed creativity, happiness and so forth. Brainstorm with yourself and write everything down.
- After running out of ideas, move clockwise a couple of steps to a different position, choose a different perspective through which to view the issue and look at the paper again. The perspective can be a 7-year-old child's perspective, the not-caring-what-people-think-about-me perspective, your pet dog's perspective, your teapot's perspective. First, write down words

which describe the item whose perspective you are looking from. The dog may be excitable, unrestricted, smelly, free and impulsive. The teapot can be a container, functional, solid, pretty, old and an heirloom.

- Now think about how this perspective sees the issue. Maybe your child perspective sees the move as a playful, fun and adventurous opportunity. The teapot may see it as being a safe, long-term investment in your future. Move around choosing multiple perspectives and thoroughly view your issue from all of them.

- Make notes and assess how you are affected within each perspective.

- Choose the most resonant perspective with which you want to view the topic and explore it further. It may be an amalgamation of a couple of them. Write out further words and phrases and divide them into two columns between emotional *being* words, such as being peaceful, calm or focused, and *action* ones such as joining a class, preparing a detailed plan or exercising regularly. The more the better.

- Now consider three things from the *being* and three things from the *doing* lists which you will say *yes* to for moving forward with your life. They can be being motivated, accepting, positive: moving home, writing your screenplay, setting up an actors group or getting up at 7.00 am every day.

- Now choose three things you will say *no* to – like being stressed, thinking too much, being diverted from your chosen career, being negative or anti-social, quitting an unpaid theatre company, saying no to alcohol and stopping drinking, hanging out with negative people.

- Then commit yourself to these tasks by doing something physical to mark it. Walk across the room, clap your hands or pat yourself on the back. Tell yourself that you have moved from the land of good intentions to the land of commitment.

- Then, obviously, follow through and stick to your commitments.

7
LEARNING SOMETHING NEW

Learning is a process.

The four stages of learning and creating new habits

As you are working on yourself and your technique, it is important to recognize that learning itself has a process. There may be times when you feel self-conscious, frustrated or annoyed that you don't get it first time, or you may decide that you don't want to do the exercises because they are not working or are taking too long. You will be pleased to know that this is all normal and that if you own this normality, you can move past it.

As highlighted in the competence theory developed by Noel Burch in the 1970s, for any skill to become second nature and unconscious, we need to go through the following four stages: unconscious incompetence, conscious incompetence, conscious competence and unconscious competence.

Let me illustrate the theory for you.

A man is driving his Jeep through the jungle when he comes across a break in the trees through which he sees a clearing and a village. He sees the native villagers going about their daily lives totally oblivious to our modern world. They are **unconsciously incompetent**. They don't know they can't drive a Jeep.

He drives into the village and, after the initial shock, in amazement and fascination the villagers gather around him and his jeep. They have never seen a man like this and don't know what the lump of metal is let alone how it is moving around by itself. They become **consciously incompetent**. They now know they can't drive a Jeep.

So, the man invites the headman of the village to learn how to drive it. He gives him a crash course (no pun intended) and when it's the headman's turn he weaves in and out of the huts struggling to come to grips with road safety and managing an automobile. He crunches the gears, stalls and does all those things that people do when learning to drive. But after a few hours practice the headman can do it, he can drive. He is delighted with himself, laughing, speeding up and slowing down at will. He becomes **consciously competent**. He now knows how to drive a Jeep and is doing it consciously.

After a hearty dinner and a good night's sleep, it becomes time for the man to leave. As he was within a day's walking distance from his initial destination, he offers to leave the Jeep for the headman to practise with and return shortly.

Upon his return a couple of days later, the man walks up to the perimeter of the village and peeks through a gap in the trees. To his great pleasure, he sees the headman nonchalantly driving around, picking things up and dropping them off, arm out the side giving lifts to other villagers. He is not thinking about driving at all, he is just doing it. He is now **unconsciously competent**.

The same process occurs when you learn anything. When you practise the exercises in this book they may feel a little uncomfortable at first and you may want to give up. But knowing this is just a phase and that you will not become unconsciously competent without first becoming consciously incompetent, may relieve the pressure of wanting to get it right.

The same is, therefore, true when engaging with and learning a new role. When you are rehearsing and consciously working on your character and relationships, waiting for them to become settled and instinctive, you will spend most of your time in the consciously incompetent/consciously competent realm. This is often uncomfortable, but it is the place where the work gets done, so is necessary. Embrace the discomfort as it is a friend of your future performance and practise until you become unconsciously competent and it becomes a habit. Aristotle roughly stated that *you are what you repeatedly do*.

In more modern times, in his book *Outliers* (2008) the writer Malcolm Gladwell looked at what makes highly successful people. Amongst others, he studied Bill Gates and successful sports teams and estimated that it takes 10,000 hours of practice to make habits. Clearly, change takes a lot of repetition and effort, and so does preparing yourself for a new role.

Believe you can develop

Great actors must possess self-awareness and self-belief. Being faithful to your strengths and weaknesses, recognizing that there is room for improvement and believing that you can work to develop your acting abilities will support you on your journey. When you have belief, your mind is open to new ideas, experiences and the effort required.

Even if you feel like an impostor there is nothing in the rule book that says you can't improve. Furthermore, without aspiration your belief will take you nowhere.

Settling for the status quo means that you have a self-limited journey which could otherwise be open, ongoing and unceasing.

What are habits and how do they form?

Habits are ritual behaviours and actions which you perform automatically. They can be good or bad, easy or hard to adopt, and simple or impossible to break. Many habits are essential so that you can walk, talk, brush your teeth and carry out almost every other behaviour you need to get you through the day. They help you recognize how you feel about people, places and things and can keep you safe or lead you to harm. Young children illustrate most clearly how one creates habits. They keep falling over until they can walk, dribble out the side of their mouths until they can eat without doing so and, relevantly, they practise accents, character and how to control their inner lives until it is ingrained in their subconscious.

If you want to be a character actor and play different people with differing features and characteristics, it is good to know your personal habits. If you find that every character you play has the same physical or vocal tic then you are not doing them justice. If you always tap the ends of your fingers when you are thinking, whether playing Joan of Arc or Lady Macbeth, then you are imposing this onto your characters rather than discovering new actions through researched exploration.

Much of what you do is dictated by habit not by choice or free will, so it makes sense that you change your bad ones if you want to develop. Without getting too scientific, research shows that the *basal ganglia* in the brain is the area which holds your habits and even when people suffer brain damage they will still maintain them if this part of the brain is left intact. So, if there is a specific place where they reside, there must be something you can do to change them by changing what goes on in this space.

The best way to remove bad habits is to create new ones and live with *them* instead. The self-help guru Tony Robbins stated that *it's really hard to change yourself, it's easy to change a pattern*.

Neuroplasticity

A way of changing patterns is aided by an understanding of neuroplasticity. Neuroscientists have identified how the brain changes when we learn something new and this can help us convert unhelpful habits into helpful ones. This is a useful asset in your own personal development, as well as your journey as an actor.

Neuroplasticity is the ability of the brain to reorganize and change itself. Reacting to stimuli around and inside you, new pathways are constantly being created in your brain and synapses fire away to create new patterns and routes as it needs. This can change the way you view what happens in the world around you, changing negative thoughts into positive ones.

If you continually walk along the same pathway you create a kind of rut, the easy way to walk, which develops into a habit and the way that you see and do things. If you constantly tell yourself that you don't have enough talent and are not good enough, that becomes a belief which is hard to shake.

Rather than trying to change or fight against your negative furrows, the solution is to start out on more positive channels instead and leave the negative ones by the wayside. For example, tell yourself that you enjoy acting and it's fun to feel challenged, or watching yourself on a screen is interesting (as opposed to frightening). The more you follow this new positive path the more the negative one becomes ignored, untended and grows over. It is still there but you are not paying any attention to it. Simply put, the best way to stop thinking about something is to think about something else instead. When a song goes around and around in your head you can stop it by singing a different one. When you begin to feel low or feel that your career has stagnated, set out on a positive road by getting out and meeting people, practising accents, singing, learning stage combat, camera technique or anything that expands your toolkit. Rather than fighting against the status quo, enjoy the journey.

Carmaker Henry Ford said that, *if you think you can, or you think you can't, you are right*. It's up to you. If you believe you can do something or get somewhere in life then you will. If you believe you can't, you won't. Hard work and technique of some description will help, but if you believe that you will become a great actor then you will become one, and if you believe that you won't, then you won't. People told Henry Ford he couldn't mass-produce automobiles, he thought he could, so he did – creating the first automobile assembly line.

Set appropriate expectations and make them stretched ones. Set reasonable timescales to achieve what you want to achieve and maintain your desire, drive and determination. You are supposed to mess up every now and again, it is to be expected. As long as it is not life-threatening it probably will not matter too much. Building better habits is not an all-or-nothing process. Don't judge or get down on yourself if you try something for a few weeks and it doesn't become routine, maybe it's supposed to take longer than that. Manage your expectations by recognizing the length of time it takes to create new behaviours. Make small incremental improvements rather than pressurizing yourself into thinking that you must do it all at once. To get to day thirty, you have to start with day one, so forget about the number and focus on the work.

As you know from the chapter on perfectionism, you don't have to be perfect. Like Edison, give yourself permission to make mistakes and embrace the process. And keep working at it as well, of course.

Hitting marks, facing the camera to let us in to your thoughts, picking up cups at the correct time, opening newspapers quietly and dropping cigarette butts are all part of the filmmaking and acting process. They must be seamless to the viewer and natural to the actor and character. You can assist in this seamlessness by dedicatedly practising at home, on the train and on the street on your way to work. If you recognize that getting it right and wrong are part of the process, and that once you get it right and practise getting it right it becomes second nature, you become unconsciously competent. You will smoothly commit to actions whilst delivering your lines and engaging in what the script requires. These actions will anchor you in, not take you out of the scene. You can drink from a coffee cup whilst stopping in front of your partner to tell them that you are leaving them, then turn away and drop the cup in a bin whilst holding back a tear.

The theory of marginal gains

The concept of marginal gains has revolutionized some sports and can change the way you approach your life as well as your acting. The theory states that small incremental improvements in any process add up to a significant improvement when they are all added together.

It is perhaps easier to understand by considering the approach of Sir Dave Brailsford. When he became performance director of British Cycling, he set about breaking down the objective of winning races into its component parts.

Brailsford believed that if it was possible to make a 1 per cent improvement in a host of areas, the cumulative gain would end up being significant. He therefore looked for all the weaknesses and latent problems in the team's routines and conventions so he could improve on each of them. For example:

- By experimenting in a wind tunnel, he noted that the test bike was not sufficiently aerodynamic.

- He discovered that dust was accumulating on the floor of the mechanic's area in the team truck, undermining bike maintenance. So he had the floor painted white to make it easier to spot any impurities.

- The team started to use antibacterial hand gel to cut down on infections.

- The riders took their own pillows from home when they were away training and riding in competition.

Each weakness was not a threat but an opportunity to create marginal gains which rapidly began to accumulate.

Team GB used to be 'also-rans' in world cycling but for the two Olympics after this strategy was implemented, they captured sixteen gold medals, and British riders won the Tour De France three times in the next four years.

If this approach can have such dramatic results in cycling, why not in acting?

EXERCISES

- Film yourself watching TV or eating dinner for a long period and observe your idiosyncrasies and habitual movements. If any habits are distracting or superfluous, break them.
- Brush your teeth with your other hand for a month. Make a diary note to remind yourself when you started and how far you have come.
- Do five small things every day for your career. The list may include buying paper clips or reading an act of a script.
- Polish your accent sentence by sentence.
- Do ten push-ups before breakfast, ten before lunch and twenty before dinner. Every day.
- Clean up your marketing materials item by item.

8
TRUST AND CREATIVITY

Trust your preparation, your instincts and yourself.

The previous chapters are redundant if you don't possess a deep trust in yourself, your creativity and your work. Trust is a certain belief in the capability, truth, power and skill of someone or something and is an essential asset for any actor. It translates into strength, ingenuity and freedom and is built by preparation and leaving yourself alone. If you trust that you have done as much work as possible in the time you have had available, your instincts will be unhindered and your performances unique and truthful.

When you let go of needing to control everything and remember that so much occurs regardless of your input, you become free and in a powerful place. You have it in your power to trust and talk to yourself in a way that has you believe you are supported and capable and that, whatever happens, you'll be OK. Creativity becomes cultivated with a permission to fail and an unattachment to the result.

If you were to write down what you have experienced and seen in your life the list would be endless. Your brain's filing cabinet of experience contains everything on this list, and if you trust that the combinations of possible outcomes are uncountable, you will never run out of creativity or become stale or wooden. Trusting your experience is liberating. If you are working with a crew you have happily worked with before, the experience will stimulate trust and shut out your saboteur's doubts.

It is this trust in yourself which brings forth your uniqueness and makes you stand out from others who would play the same role. It is impossible that two people can play the same part in exactly the same way and this knowledge removes the pressure to *get it right*. You get it right for *you*. Some actors with the Impostor Syndrome fear they are inadequate and not interesting enough but it is your idiosyncrasies which make you different and interesting, not boring or like everyone else.

Strive for creativity. Believe you have it and let it pass through you. If you judge your creativity rather than *be* it then it cannot exist. Picasso didn't *try* to be creative. *Trying* to do something dilutes the power of trust. He prepared with sketches before committing his ideas to canvas and he didn't have the burden of *doing it right*.

Trust may sometimes make the job seem too easy but, combined with preparation, it should be. A jumbo jet pilot flying at 30,000 feet comes across challenges, but the process and technicalities of flying are easy to him. He is in the moment and when an incident arises – as when it does for your characters in a scene – he flies on instinct and uses everything he has learned to right the situation. He may feel fear but will only reflect upon it after the event. He does not have time to be afraid or check in with his feelings, he just experiences and rides along the top of his experience. Which is the same for you as an actor.

Instinct is how you naturally react or behave without having to learn about it beforehand. Some behaviours are a combination of instinct and learned behaviour, but others happen without any teaching at all; like a baby's need to feed or the instinct to run when you see a hungry bear coming towards you.

An actor can only really experience instinct with trust. When it comes to living truthfully within a scene, you must trust your instincts. Talent comes from instincts and you can't pretend to react to them, you just react without thinking. As Meisner says throughout much of his work, intellect has nothing to do with acting.

It is not sufficient to merely trust *yourself*, though, and it helps immensely if you trust those around you. If you trust that your director has a vision outside and above your scene then it is easier to take his direction. If you don't trust them and fight their ideas or mope around the set grumbling and complaining to anyone who will listen it does not help. Accept your position as a participant in their artistic venture, do your job and find a way to trust them. Make their notes truthful for yourself and leave all other issues aside.

The same is true with your fellow actors. They may not be able to act but an evident lack of trust in them will hinder both your performances. Trust yourself enough and the rest of it shouldn't matter.

When you trust that you can ride the bike, jump out of the plane, remember the four-page monologue, deliver an intimate emotional speech in front of a crew of seventy-five whilst sitting semi-naked on a freezing cold park bench, all will be well. It is this trusting yourself, allied to your focus and concentration, which will prove your worth as an actor and give you confidence enough to be re-employable.

Trust and confidence go hand-in-hand and build one upon the other like a snowball collecting snow as it rolls down a hill. But the opposite is also true. A lack of trust being allowed to fester has the potential to breed insecurity and a shortened career.

The list of whom and what to trust is endless. Write your own in your notebook, but here are a few to get you started:

Trust list

- your creativity
- the script
- the director
- the crew
- your fellow cast
- your own ability
- your senses
- your experience
- your personality
- your audience
- that every take will be different no matter how many you do

PART THREE

AS YOU ARE MOVING TOWARDS SOMEONE ELSE

9

SCREEN EXPERIENCE

Be comfortable in front of the camera.

A limiting belief which many actors put in their own way is that they lack experience in front of a camera. Whether they have worked on one short film or twenty-five features, there is often a belief that it is not enough. This can feed into the Impostor Syndrome and saboteur and result in an unbalancing of the inner actor/inner character mix (see later chapter). Nasty.

Fear of the camera is clearly a major hindrance for any screen actor. If you freeze or start shaking every time you stand or sit in front of one, then you won't get much work and your screen career will undoubtedly be short. However, this perceived lack of experience is a matter of perspective, perception and attitude and the remedy could be as simple as a switch between one view and another.

Let me illustrate what I mean with the following two examples.

Firstly, if you are reading this book in a public place you are probably on camera at this very moment. If you are reading it at home after a long day outside, then you have probably been on camera around one hundred times since you left the house this morning. If you have just got up and are reading it over your breakfast table, you had better get ready for your close-up. Either way, you have been on camera thousands and thousands of times in your life.

Yes folks, I'm talking about closed-circuit television or, as it is more commonly known, CCTV.

The Western world is flooded with CCTV cameras and there are 6 million in the UK alone. In the United States, it was reported in 2009 that there were 30 million surveillance cameras shooting 4 billion hours of footage a week. This doesn't even consider the satellites which are constantly recording us.

Being on CCTV doesn't require years of training or worrying that your eyebrow moves too much or that you are frowning. You generally don't notice that it is there or change your behaviour because of it (unless you are up to no good, of course); demonstrating that if you are not thinking about the camera or being scrutinized by it you can and do behave *normally*.

Of course, as an actor, there is more to it. If you are on TV or in a film, there is usually a script. The script is what makes the interaction dramatic or comedic and gives it purpose, rather than just a couple of people chatting. It's what keeps the story moving and worth engaging with. The script will help you work out who you are, what you are doing and how you will do it. You will be standing in front of, walking past, towards or away from the camera with a purpose that someone somewhere has designated for you.

I will talk later about learning lines but if you are so off book that the lines are not an issue and you are very clear on who you are, what you want and what you are doing, then there is no space for your inner character to be impacted by an over-attentive inner actor. If you have worked hard enough on the character and the script, and are thinking the character's thoughts, then you will not notice or concern yourself with the camera. It's as if you are in a documentary.

Secondly, you have undoubtedly been photographed and recorded hundreds of times by friends and family on their camera phones. There is footage of genuine laughter and tears, of surprises, shocks, and truthful reactions to events and the world around you. It can be pleasing and entertaining to watch someone who has been captured in a moment and there will also be instances of overacting and *performing* when you know you are being recorded. It is likely that you were initially self-conscious, but the more you were filmed this way, the more comfortable you became.

My point is that you are no novice. You have camera experience, awareness and sense. You know where one is positioned and can ignore it if you are concentrating on something else. So, do that. Concentrate on your character's life instead of thinking that the camera can see what a fraud you are. There is a camera in front of you but it is just another piece of the furniture.

One of the differences between screen and stage acting is that with stage acting you may need to show people what you think, feel and do. You go to them. However, with screen acting your job is to experience life and let the camera observe and pick it up. So, the viewer comes to you. Allow them to formulate their own view on what you are thinking based on their subjective experiences of life and understanding of the action in that moment. Live it, don't show it.

EXERCISE

For the next week look out for as many CCTV cameras as you can; in shops, on the train, walking down the street, standing in the bank, going to a sporting event, the theatre or just about anything and anywhere else.

Notice how self-conscious you feel when you think about the camera looking at you and that there is someone somewhere possibly watching your every move and making judgements on you. Notice how, as the week progresses, this becomes less and less important and you become more relaxed being *on camera.*

Make a diary note for a month's time to remind yourself that you have been on camera more than a thousand times since you began the exercise. Remind yourself that you acted *normally.*

EXERCISE

Set your camera facing you, press record and notice the little red light (if it has one). Think consciously of the camera observing you and how everyone will watch the footage later.

Keep the camera rolling and think about what you did the previous evening. Go through all the events, considering the sights and sounds you experienced. After at least a minute switch back to looking at the camera. Then cut and review. Reflect upon how you forgot about the camera once you focused on something else and notice the difference in your eyes and the muscles of your face.

10
FOCUS AND CONCENTRATION

Develop your focus and concentration. Get in the scene and stay in it.

From childhood, you have been told to focus and concentrate. Focus and concentrate otherwise you will never finish your dinner, get dressed or learn anything at school. Focus on your career. Concentrate on your driving, on the safety instructions on board the plane and on the beginning of the movie or you will miss the plot.

Having been drummed into you so often and for so long, focusing and concentrating must have become habits by now. Mustn't they? Unfortunately, however, it is often still a battle and, if you have had to read a badly written script from cover to cover in one sitting, you'll know what I mean.

But does it really matter?

If you are a surgeon performing a triple bypass, in a medical theatre – rather than a performance one – then focus and concentration are essential not just for you, but for the life of another human being. Acting is, obviously, not so life and death, but the need to focus and concentrate is still important.

Focus is doing one thing without distraction and is what allows you to start, perform and finish a task. It helps you concentrate and keep your head, while all about you others are losing theirs. It is very easy to get distracted in life and on a set it is even easier. Film sets may often be chaotic places with legions of people diligently, and often noisily, carrying out their own individual functions within the greater organism. On an average-sized professional set you have your fellow actors, the director and a whole host of production people – including line producers, production assistants, production managers, assistant production managers, unit managers, production coordinators, first and second (at least) assistant directors, location manager, assistant location manager, continuity and script supervisors, director of photography, camera operator, first assistant camera operator (focus puller), clapper loader, film loader, gaffer, best boy, various other lighting technicians, electrical, grips, dolly grip, sound recordist, boom operator, art department, carpenter, props, costume department, hair and makeup, catering and so on and so forth. Phew! It's tiring just typing this. But you must concentrate amidst intense, emotional and physical circumstances and remain specific, calm and professional.

Focus and concentration could be synonyms for discipline. Discipline to create, believe and maintain that the woman with a knife chasing you through a crowded shopping mall is really your wife; or the man walking up the steps of the gallows amid hundreds of baying spectators is really your husband. Imagination is necessary but there is a need for it to be focused and disciplined otherwise your performance may become confused and erratic.

Focus does not have to be a narrow attention on something. You can focus on saving the world just as you can focus on a cell under a microscope. Sometimes the whole world is small and sometimes it is large. Sometimes, like when defusing a nuclear bomb, it is wise to exclude everything outside your point of focus; whilst sometimes, as when in the middle of a pride of lions, it is not – if you're only focusing on what is happening in front you may miss the peripheral vision and get pounced on and eaten. As an actor, the sensation of focus on this 360-degree awareness will allow you to be truly alive in the moment of the scene. It's that sensation when you are talking to somebody in front of you whilst someone threatening or protective is standing next to or just behind you. You sense their energy and it impacts on how you feel and talk. If you are arguing with someone on the street and feel the crowd behind you is on your side, you will have greater confidence than if you don't notice they are there. Each of the *Magnificent Seven* gained confidence walking down Main Street with the knowledge that the other six were somewhere close (Sturges, 1960).

Concentration is more general and broad than focus but the need to concentrate is also an essential component of your job as an actor. Whether preparing for your role at home, in the rehearsal room or in your trailer, you must concentrate. If you are learning your lines and are constantly being distracted by putting the kettle on, checking Facebook and writing emails, the likelihood of you being ready when needed to be will be diminished.

It may not always be possible to find a suitable quiet space to prepare so you must learn to concentrate with everything happening around you. It is like playing a video game where, if you lose concentration for a nano-second, it's game over. Except, on a movie set, there can be more at stake as other people's work is affected. In movies such as *Dunkirk* or *Saving Private Ryan*, everything is meticulously set up with multiple cameras, explosions and action all over the place. So, any fluff of your lines or lack of concentration could have a catastrophic impact. If they have already blown up a huge chunk of the beach, it will not be appreciated if you are not on your mark when they press the detonator for the next series of explosions.

Being concentrated and focused also saves time and can relieve your anxiety. Knowing and accepting that you have prepared as much as was possible in the time you have had available, will help you focus on character rather than inner actor considerations.

Focus and concentration are considered a given and everyone expects it of you. You must show up prepared. Other things do draw our attention and there may be someone behind the camera scratching their nose or doing push-ups, but it is expected that you keep on point and stay with it.

There is a difference between focusing and staring, of course. It is often stated that acting is about looking the other person in the eye and talking, but people don't stare in real life; or if they do it is being done for a specific response. Anyone who stares all the time could rightly be regarded as weird.

Reframing it as being curious rather than rigidly concentrating may allow the interaction to become a more relaxed and pleasant journey rather than a pressurized destination. Trust your curiosity and permit it to go where it will. In rehearsal, set the curiosity animal off on its journey and, *on the day,* allow the character to use curiosity to explore what they and the other characters want and need.

A great deal of research has been conducted on focus, concentration and attention, including by psychologist Richard Wiseman. In one of his experiments (Wiseman, 2004), viewers of a video of people in black or white T-shirts passing basketballs to each other were asked to count the times the players with white T-shirts passed the ball to each other. As they became engrossed in their task, a person in a gorilla suit walked through the court and through the frame. The viewers were asked how many passes were made, then who spotted the gorilla? Eighty per cent of the respondents did not notice it. They were so focused on the task they had been given that they did not see something which was so out of place. They became blind to the unexpected even when they were staring right at it. This is known as *inattention blindness* and is the reason why many drivers crash their cars while talking on the phone. Whilst focus and concentration are essential in your life and your career, make sure that you don't miss what else is going on around you. On a macro level, don't miss the opportunities in life which present themselves, and on a micro one, don't miss the opportunities which present themselves to your characters in their imaginary circumstances. As John Lennon put it, *life is what happens while you're busy making other plans* (Lennon, 1980).

Milestones and anchors

There will be times when you lose concentration and drop out of a scene. This is normal, but instead of disappearing down a rabbit hole of despair you can refocus and regain concentration by using milestones and anchors.

As on a road, a milestone is a point within a scene which you must reach and pass to ensure that you/it move forward in the intended direction of travel. This landmark may take the form of a specific action, thought, beat change, or reference to an event or person outside of the scene. When reading the script and preparing your role, look for these important milestones and, once identified, hand the information over to your inner actor to store in your mind's filing cabinet (see later chapter on Inner Actor and Inner Character). If you then need it, your inner actor will shoot off a distress flare to your information retrieval bank for help, receive the backup file and hand it over to the inner character.

In the movie *Kramer vs Kramer* (Benton, 1979), Joanna and Ted, the estranged couple in the title, meet in a restaurant after a long time apart and talk about their son Billy. Billy is not in the scene in person but they both have a specific, powerful and solid image with which to ground them into what is happening. If either actor's focus slips and they are no longer fully in, the reference to Billy can pull their character back and refocus them. Seeing his face, thinking of his smile, or a phrase he always uses becomes a powerful hook, milestone and anchor. The online Google dictionary states that an anchor is *a person or thing which provides stability or confidence in an otherwise uncertain situation*. Stability and confidence can be reinforced by this specific physical, mental or sensory point; like a stake in the ground (or scene). Let me illustrate what I mean.

I was shooting on a set with a large and animated crew who were bustling around setting up for following shots, dressing the set and the actors and preparing for lunch. My action was very simple; I had to go into a shed, find my bicycle, decide if I wanted to ride it then dust it off. This sounds straightforward practically but the skill comes in hitting the same physical and mental level for every one of the 40-odd takes we shot (what with different lenses, angles, setups, etc).

I noticed a yellow and green slug pellet container on the shelf in the shed and used it as an anchor and point of focus to reset to the same place. Every time the first AD called the set to order, ready to roll, I brought myself back to my base by focusing on that container. And every time the take was usable.

Focus can also be established and maintained by preparing the mental and physical journey prior to the scene in your preparation. If you prepare and go through the last few minutes of your mental and physical journey to the point of *action* then the hullabaloo around you will be blocked out. Close your eyes and be on the bus ride to the house, see yourself walk from the stop to the gate, push the gate and walk up the path, pause at the door then ring the bell. While you are engaged in this, the make-up person is doing last looks and applying powder and the clapper board is being thrust in front of your face whilst people shout scene numbers, final comments and announcements. And you are where you need to be; focused, ready and able.

To help reach this nirvana, you need to train your focus and concentration. Like everything else it demands work, but this doesn't have to be hard work and it can even be enjoyable.

EXERCISE

Look at the sense memory exercises in the *senses* chapter, starting with the breakfast drink, and focus and concentrate on them.

EXERCISE

Find a particularly noisy place such as a building site, train station or road and learn a page of text. Test yourself by dropping in and out of concentration, noticing and then ignoring what is going on around you.

EXERCISE

Read a screenplay from beginning to end in one sitting. Distractions will come into your head but don't do anything about them. Yes, you may have to buy some milk or call a friend or book a show but don't do it yet. If you need, keep a notepad by your side and make notes, but stick to the task in hand.

Repeat the task with a different screenplay.

Not only is this good for concentration, but it is also beneficial for your craft and career and satisfying as a job well done.

EXERCISE

Focus on one visual object. Then do something/anything else, such as listening to the radio, reading a sentence of a magazine or looking out the window. Then focus on the object again, then on anything else, then on the object and so forth; like doing repetitions at the gym.

11
EMOTIONS

Identify, understand and manipulate your emotions.

An emotion is a strong feeling or response triggered by an event or relationship. The generation of an emotion directs your mind to search its filing cabinet for viable solutions and remedies which then stimulate instincts, impulses, and actions. You witness a clown falling over, remember that this is supposed to be funny then respond with a throaty guffaw or chuckle. Or not.

Emotion is a result of something else, some other stimulus. We witness a child getting run over so feel pain and sorrow. We see a character sleeping with their best friend's partner and have a reaction based on who we are at that moment in our life. I may get angry, you may get turned on.

When you were young you were told to manipulate your emotions. You were told to cheer up, calm down, don't be so happy. If it were that simple we would be living in a *Stepford Wives* or *Truman Show* world where everything is squeaky clean and aggression is very short lived and easily overcome. But you did learn how to manipulate different emotions in different situations for your own ends; as I can attest to watching my children sweetly smiling when they want an ice cream, swiftly followed by screaming in anger and grief, and pleading in desperation when their original tactic hasn't worked.

Your emotions have a significant impact on who you are, what you do and how you are perceived and you need to be in tune with and manipulate them for performance and fidelity to the script. You manipulate them to influence others and attain an emotional response from them. Your character may cry to elicit guilt in your scene partner to force them to change their behaviour.

We watch movies and TV and go to the theatre to be moved; to feel something and to be affected by the lives of the characters within the imaginary world. You must allow the viewer to decide how they feel and not impose your emotions upon them, but you must feel them all the same.

Interesting acting requires you to control your emotions. To be a colourful actor with a long and varied range of parts it is likely you will need a long list of varied and easily available emotions. In life, you may find it hard to love, get angry or laugh, but in your job, you must be able to readily exercise them. You also need to have control over them to keep to the story rather than a rambling series of possibly unconnected emotional outbursts.

Many actors believe that acting is all about emotions. They believe that they should go around *feeling* things and that if they feel and show them then that is enough and they are doing a superb job. Three points:

1. In real life people go around hiding their emotions not showing them.
2. We experience multiple and different emotions at the same time.
3. People who go around showing their emotions all the time risk being friendless or locked up.

Often, the best way to create an impact on an audience is to not show your emotions but keep them hidden under the waterline. Many of your characters are actually trying to keep control. When you see someone holding back their tears it is more powerful than if they are self-indulgently blubbing all over the place. The former makes you sympathize/empathize whilst the latter makes you want to run away.

We keep our emotions to ourselves with the truth often hidden. Of course, it has to be there or your performance will be empty and fake, and, as no philosopher has ever said, *if there is nothing happening underneath the waterline then it is not an iceberg*.

If you know that your partner has something up on you, you may appear stronger by seeming unaffected. In *Stepmom* (Columbus, 1998), for example, the protagonists are engaged in a tug of war for our heartstrings. We sympathize with both Julia Roberts' character as well as Susan Sarandon's. If the balance is tipped too far either way for too long they will lose both the battle with the characters around them and us as observers. They need to hold back their true feelings, fears and doubts as much as possible to make the film work. The viewer will sympathize more if you resist the tears and suffer internally.

Showing everything may go against the movie as a whole. The script and the music are there to do much of the work for you if you let them. The music is often an extra character influencing the viewer's opinions and mood. The underscore may be very sad violin music and if you weep and wail with abandon the scene may lose its impact.

The Magdalene Sisters (Mullan, 2002) is moving because of the girls' stories, not the tears they shed. The way they stand up to, or give in to, the harsh lives they are forced to endure moves us and directs our emotions to soften and harden and rise and fall. If the actors tried to show us how tough life is for them it simply would not have worked. I feel for them from a distance due to *my* view of social justice not *theirs*.

As an actor, you will have a deep curiosity of what is going on with the other characters, how they are behaving and what they *really* want. They may be displaying anger, but your exploration uncovers their sorrow. You may have to work harder to get to their truth when they appear emotionally closed or unavailable.

This sharing of information varies with the nature and length of our relationships. If you have just met a potential life partner you may show different strengths of the same emotions than if you have been married for thirty years. If you have never met the other character you will display different shades of emotions than if they were your sibling.

We have learnt to cover our emotions and very often it has become an automatic response. There is equally a learned way of detecting the signals in others. We spot micro signals such as flaring nostrils or a very slight grinding of the teeth. Set responses for specific emotions have been developed over the centuries and we respond in common ways. Many of your characters will be hiding such strong responses that you need to learn how to manipulate and keep your emotions to yourself.

You need to affect your emotional responses and your reactions to them. You need skill and tools to understand, gauge, pitch and control them. Viewers do not want to/cannot watch two hours of shouting, laughing or crying. They need a journey which includes respite and times to reflect. You do not need to hit the nail on the head and if you control yourself and resist showing every emotion that you think the character feels, you will be able to manipulate them more effectively. Let the viewer make their own mind up how they feel about something.

There are also cultural aspects to consider. The British are generally more reserved and less demonstrative than your average American and don't like to display or talk about how they feel. Gender-wise, men and women are expected to feel and react in different ways and if it is not as we expect then we have a different reaction to them. The script should dictate this.

We often experience more than one emotion at a time and you should be careful interpreting them in yourself and others. We feel shades of grey, extremes and multiple emotions based on who we are, where we have come from and what we are experiencing.

You can love and hate simultaneously or be surprised and angry at something you have done. You can find humour in the face of fear. The strongest drama has conflicting emotions concurrently present, as in *Othello* where the title character kills the one he loves due to jealousy.

Consequently, the note *play this emotion* or *that emotion* is very limiting and constraining. Emotion is not precise, so if it is imprecise how can you act it? You cannot show, indicate, express or fabricate one, you can only feel it, and by feeling it, react to it or choose not to. In real life, you don't *try* to be emotional. It must come from a place of truth and if you *try* to laugh or cry it comes out all wrong and looks as fake as it is. If the circumstances are funny for us then we will laugh. This relieves the pressure of *getting it right*. Did I feel *exactly* how my character would in this situation?

The way an emotion is displayed differs from person to person and from character to character. Each of us laughs, cries and shouts differently. I keep my anger in while my daughter stamps her feet and bares her teeth.

When the director asks us to be happier or sadder what does that mean and how can you do it? It is impossible to gauge exactly what he or she wants. What then happens is that you try to achieve this emotion on a hit or miss basis and as you are approaching the part where you are supposed to feel sad you become overly conscious and the inner actor takes over and judges what you are doing. You then drop out and have to find ways of getting back in and the overriding emotion becomes overacted. A good director may make a sensitive adjustment based on what is going on rather than a scale of 1 to 10 on the emotions barometer. If they don't help with the adjustment, work out for yourself what is causing you this emotion. If the scene involves you recognizing that you have lost your family, your home and money and that there is no escape from this mire, then sadness, anger and fear may come in and out in differing combinations and strengths. Prepare with thoughts of your happiness and examples of when times were good, then take them away and feel the results and the consequences. This way you will experience the loss rather than intellectually superimposing it on your circumstances. Feel the loss in the given circumstances and your emotional response will be appropriate, or at the least, acceptable in its truth and a good starting point. Set up the circumstances, get out of your own way and trust yourself that what comes will be right.

The same is true when deciding in advance that your character is feeling a certain emotion at a certain time – see the section on *the potential limitations of objectives and actioning* in the chapter Improvise and Personalize. In the moment of the action, you may not actually feel sad, but anger tinged with a hint of sadness and a smidgen of resignation.

If you decide on an emotion in advance you cut off all other opportunities. 'cide' at the end of a word allows no further exploration: suicide, genocide, patricide, decide. Once you decide how it's going to be, you paint yourself into a corner and reduce the chances of actually experiencing what your character is experiencing. What results is intellectual acting from the neck up without the possibility of a journey down into your body.

Research on how many base emotions there are is divided, but the general consensus is a minimum of between four and eight, which include happiness, sadness, surprise, anger and fear. Aristotle points to anger, calmness, joy, fear, courage, shame, confidence, kindness, cruelty, pity, indignation, envy/jealousy, love and hate. Of course, there are also subcategories, so when a director asks you to be sad on a certain line, you have to figure out which subcategory they are looking for and how strongly they want you to pitch it. It is important to know the reasons and triggers of why you are sad or angry in the scene and understand how much you do or don't want to show the other characters.

An emotion is more easily noticeable through the face. When someone is boiling with rage the blood flows to the skin and muscles, and micro movements and colour are all heightened and identifiable by others. The opposite is true with fear when the blood leaves the face and makes it white. When love is in the air, the mouth, nose, eyes and eyebrows are all positioned differently still.

In *Expression of the Emotions in Man and Animals* (1872), Charles Darwin states that emotions are behavioural traits which have evolved and our faces have adapted to display them. He lists suffering, anxiety, grief, dejection, despair, joy, love, devotion, bad temper, determination, hatred, anger, disdain, contempt, disgust, guilt, pride, surprise, fear, terror, shame and shyness amongst others.

Pushing and indicating – trying too hard

Pushing occurs when the actor is not truly and truthfully feeling the emotions and circumstances but tries to show the viewer that they are. The logic is that, by helping the viewer recognize what is going on, they will feel the same way too. This is also true when you don't like or understand the script and try to make it more interesting than you think it is. As previously stated, however, this is not advisable, as if you don't believe it then neither will anybody else.

There are many obvious pitfalls to pushing and indicating and it is to be avoided at all costs. If you are pushing the emotion then your brain will be saying to you, *what the hell is going on? Why are they doing that? I think I'll drop out and let them do it on their own.* Essentially, you become *unconnected.*

Beware, also, of playing exclamation marks. You don't know exactly how strong, or in what way, the writer wanted your character to exclaim so you will stymie yourself by attempting to match it. The temptation may be to shout rather than intensely mutter under your breath, because that is what the exclamation mark means!!!

Affective memory

Luckily, we can influence our emotions. We can calm ourselves down, control our lust and stop hysterically laughing in inappropriate situations. The good news for you as an actor is that when you are not feeling inspired by the material, rather than faking it, you can use technique and intentionally introduce intense emotions into your work. Using events retrieved from your memory banks, you can trigger genuine emotional responses in the moment. Lee Strasberg called it *affective memory* or *emotional recall.*

Affective memory is the retrieval and reliving of a previous event which generates an accompanying positive or negative response, like rage, deep pain or hysterical laughter. Obviously, when working, the ideal is to be inspired, but this may not always be possible and you may have to control the creative mood. You may find it hard to repeat the same (ish) emotions take after take or night after night and you may need some help when you feel uninspired or when you cannot viscerally relate to the events in the script. For instance, if the script has your wife and kids killed in a car crash and you are not a family man and cannot truly relate, you can use a memory which, at the time, had as powerful a response – maybe your goldfish dying when you were 6? I found a letter in my mother's room when I was about 8 or 9 which had a very intense impact on me at the time. Now, in retrospect, it has no impact at all as such. But when I sensorially return to the place, the smells, the sounds and tastes, the deeply powerful emotion comes flooding back. This can then be connected to the events of the scene to make the emotional response real *and* appropriate.

In *The Godfather III* (Coppola, 1990), when his screen daughter is shot outside the opera, Al Pacino must dig deep down to a real and intensely human place to make the scene work. I don't know how many set-ups, angles and takes he had but if it were more than a couple then it may have been difficult to reach the required pitch every time. He would undoubtedly have worked on the naked truth of a highly emotional situation and incorporated it into the action.

There is a powerful synthesis between the actor and their role and, as it is consciously created by the actor rather than a chance meeting, affective memory can strengthen this bond. The technique is useful in rehearsal to find an emotional space in which your character may be living. Work on the exercise by yourself and bring it to rehearsal ready to go; the rest of your cast will probably not want to sit around waiting for you to finish working on a personal exercise.

It is recommended that the events you work on occurred longer than seven years ago as your association with them will be more stable. Also, they will not affect relationships in your present life as the energy will have lessened over time.

EXERCISE

Pick an event from your past, older than seven years, which was, at the time, hugely emotional, and work on it in the following way:

- Split the exercise into two parts – leading up to the event, and the event itself. Take a lot of time and go through the lead up many times in order to strongly and clearly establish it. I would recommend a few days as the more stable the circumstances, the more controllable the output.

- Make yourself comfortable, close your eyes and breathe gently in and out. Remember back to the place you were in when the incident occurred and, in your mind's eye, slowly look around and take in what you see. Then use your other senses to ground yourself in the place and slowly allow the incident to come closer. Then stop, go back and start again.
- When the pre-events are clear, you may get to the event itself. Allow yourself the freedom to experience it again all these years later in the knowledge that it is just an exercise and you can release yourself from it when you have finished. But really experience and immerse yourself in it.
- After the *moment of impact,* stay within the moment and allow a small part of your inner actor to gently observe what is happening and how you feel.
- Practise again as you wish.

See https://vimeo.com/251793609 for an example.

EXERCISE

- Write out a list of emotions.
- Find and set triggers for each, giving more background and context as to what makes you feel that emotion.
- Focus on those triggers and experience the emotion.
- Notice what happens, how easy or hard it is to achieve the emotion, how clear or vague and so forth.
- Work on those emotions which you find harder to access until they become easier.

12
IMAGINATION

I am enough of an artist to draw freely upon my imagination. Imagination is more important than knowledge. Knowledge is limited. Imagination encircles the world.

ALBERT EINSTEIN

Imagination is the creation and manipulation in your mind of new images, sensations, actions, ideas and worlds. Unless you are playing yourself in your own story, you will need to invent experiences, events, people, places and things. To be real and believable you will need a strong enough imagination to convince yourself, and therefore the viewer, that these imaginary circumstances are real. If you do not then the story has no context, truth or drama.

Consider the power of your own imagination. The clearest example is a nightmare. You were chased over a cliff by a fire-breathing dragon, your mind and body believed it and the fight/flight feeling stays with you for the rest of the day as if it really happened. Your brain convinces you that it did happen, and your body and emotions follow its lead. Similarly, by powerfully imagining your inner character's experiences (see later chapter), the events in the script can become tangible and you can make them so real that you believe you are experiencing them. As Pablo Picasso stated, *everything you can imagine is real*.

Imagination is linked to the senses. To imagine a dirty street in Caracas it helps if you hear the noise, smell the street, taste the grime in your mouth and feel the dirt on your skin. If you sensorially create a new world and place this in your brain as real, you will be able to access it when needed in your performance. If your senses are not being utilized and are not telling the truth to your brain, the knife being waved in front of you will just be the piece of plastic you know it is and you will, therefore, not be genuinely afraid of it.

You were born with an imagination and used it to its fullest until you were told by your elders and betters that it is childish and not what an adult does. Which clearly doesn't make sense. It is an imagination which realized and created the Taj Mahal, the Houses of Parliament and the Golden Gate Bridge. And where would the world be without Disneyland?

As a craftsperson, it is important to have easy access to your imagination as one of the tools of your trade and you can exercise and train yours to make the results more vivid and accessible. Your imagination must be so rich and powerful that you can shut out the outside world when you need, leaving only you, your fellow cast members and the imagined world within which you all exist. You can train your imagination to see right through the camera equipment in front of you and view the ocean behind it, or look up and see the solar system through the ceiling of the set above your head. You can look into a camera lens and believe that you are studying yourself in a mirror, or that the tape on the side of the camera is your lover.

Your imagination draws you into the reality and immediacy of a scene and keeps you in it. Imagining sounds in your head when on a silent set, talking loudly over music which isn't there but will be superimposed later, hearing the roar of lions of a piece of music by Chopin, the march of jackboots or the sound of birdsong are services you may well be asked to employ. These sounds will affect what you are feeling, thinking and doing, will nuance your performance and help the viewers gauge their own pitch at which they feel the story. So, you must really hear it and not fake it.

Your imagination will affect your behaviour. If you strongly imagine that you have an aversion to meeting people, you may withdraw when someone approaches you. If you imagine that you love women with large noses you may very well stare at them on the street. You can add contrived memories to believe that something made up has actually transpired. You may not have had children but can close your eyes and dream that you hear their little voices as they run around your imaginary home playing their own imaginary games.

Freud, the founder of psychoanalysis, talked about the subconscious as being a storage area of experiences and memories. He stated that we may not even know that these memories are there let alone the impact they have on our day to day behaviour. But they are there and as a self-aware actor you can use them for the benefit of your characters and the stories they need to tell. Spontaneity and creativity comes from, and is used by, the ocean of information stored and indexed within your mind. It is what makes you *you* and allows you to create individual and unique characters and behaviours. The list of character questions in Appendix 5 will feed into this store, and when you absorb the information the result cannot be anything else but real, immediate and present. Because your imagination can believe and own this homework, it will be lived as real life once the camera starts rolling.

The power of the imagination must be controlled of course. If you are in a long-running show it is important to exist outside of your character even if they are very close in personality to yourself. Your research and preparation must also be finite otherwise you will spend the rest of your life being that other person and everyone in your own life whom you hold dear will disappear.

As highlighted in the previous chapter, when using affective memory, memories from your real life take you to places where strong emotions lie.

However, sometimes you will need to go deeper than you have experienced. This is where fantasy and imagination can help. You can have a traumatic memory of Tiddles the cat being run over at a young age and super enhance it by imagining his slaughter along with other cats at the hands of a megalomaniacal cat hating tyrant.

Einstein stated that your imagination is limitless. You can shrink to the size of a pea and travel by ship into the ear canal, jet off into space alongside a partner who looks rather like a bear and speaks a weird language, or drown in a sea of magma only to resurface in time for lunch.

J. G. Ballard said: *I believe in the power of the imagination to remake the world, to release the truth within us, to hold back the night, to transcend death, to charm motorways, to ingratiate ourselves with birds, to enlist the confidences of madmen* (Ballard, 1984).

Carl Sagan added: *Imagination will often carry us to worlds that never were, but without it we go nowhere* (Sagan, 1980).

EXERCISE

Review the method-based exercises in the chapter on the senses and concentrate on transforming real people, places and objects into fantasy ones. A pen may become a snake, your friend may become the big bad wolf and your sister may become Hillary Clinton.

EXERCISE

Wherever you are reading this, look around and take in your surroundings. Be free, steer clear of your judgemental head and allow your imagination to wander. Allow the environment to change and see where you end up. Maybe you are in a harem in the desert or in a prison cell with the walls closing in on you. As your imagination wanders further it is possible that other senses may join in the journey. The smells of incense and the touch of silk in the harem may relax you and make you feel sensual.

When the vision is vivid enough notice how your mood/emotions may have been impacted. It is possible that walls closing in may make you tense and increase your heart rate; or the magic potion in your goblet may affect you in a range of ways.

EXERCISE

Watch people on the street, the train and in cafes and make up stories about them. Have a strong opinion on who they are and what they are up to. Reconnect with your inner child and feel no boundaries. Maybe they are spies, big businessmen sealing a deal or master criminals on the run? Imagine they are thinking of splitting with partners or that they are writing novels in their heads – and imagine what the novel is about. Where are they going? Why did they take the train today and not drive in their chauffer driven limo?

13
LISTENING

Listening is at least as important as talking. You have two ears and one mouth, use them in that proportion.

Listening is an active and responsive process. You listen to spoken and unspoken communication, take in and absorb language, body language and true intention, and unconsciously assess and analyse what the other person is saying and doing. Then, through the filter of your experience, you make decisions on how you will react.

It is often said that acting is listening, that the scene is about the other person and all you must do is listen and respond. However, this is a little simplistic as it does not consider a whole host of other circumstances, such as events outside the scene which the other character may be unaware of. If you are listening and nothing else, you are encouraged to stare at each other because this is what listening supposedly looks like.

But listening is not staring or 100 per cent focusing on every syllable the other person utters. When we listen to people in life we don't stare at them. In some cultures, it is actually rude to look the other person in the eye for protracted periods of time. Observe people talking to each other and you will see that they rarely maintain eye contact. They look up when they are thinking and down when they are remembering; or is it the other way around? I think it may even be the opposite for left-handed people.

Listening is observing micro movements and sensing what the other person is putting in front of you. Blind people develop heightened hearing and listening and can pick up on many nuances, mistruths or misdirections which non-visually impaired people may not. They focus more on the communication than on other distractions.

Listening isn't the same as hearing. Hearing is a physical activity where sounds enter your ears. It is passive, and the sounds are received automatically without much input. Listening is more active and involves you in focusing and concentrating on the act of communication: the words, actions, physicality and energy.

Research by psychologist Albert Mehrabian (1971) explored how communication occurs between humans. Whilst his research has been questioned, the essential principles are significant. He found that 55 per cent of communication is in the body language, 38 per cent in the tone, intonation and volume of the voice, and only the remaining 7 per cent in the words. Essentially, listening is bigger than just words passing through the ears, and it ain't what you do, it's the way that you do it.

Listening is not a passive process. In fact, the listener should be at least as engaged in the process as the speaker. The phrase *active listening* is used to describe this process of being fully involved. The camera loves to see actors listening and actively reacting. Watch your favourite films and TV programmes and you will notice that the editor and director hold on the listener for their reactions more than the speaker.

For some people, listening is where they are waiting for others to stop talking so they can start. They hear them, but it doesn't really have an impact.

For others, listening is more attentive. There is a sharper attention on the other person and you observe their body language and the way they are saying what they are saying. However, you only see and hear them but don't use your sixth sense, your intuition.

The ideal form of listening for actors and laypeople alike is more comprehensive. You use all your senses as well as your instincts and their relationship with their environment. You pick up on observable, intuitive signals, which enable you to notice the effects your words are having on the listener; how they land and what you can then do about their reaction. In this way of thinking, listening is not just with your ears and you are more present. It is that type of concentration which becomes so intense that it can sometimes be exhausting.

When you are fully listening, there is no space for the inner actor. If you have prepared for your inner character, you will be so focused on your surroundings and what fills them that you cannot get distracted by inconsequentialities. If you prepare your role carefully, taking into account the opinions, history and thoughts of your character, listening happens quickly and your thoughts will also be quick. You will not be picking up on line cues but on the impulses which are generated from listening to the spoken and unspoken words. The cues become a deep connection rather than superficially waiting for your turn. Truly living in the moment allows spontaneity and listening allows the scene to feel like an improvisation.

Sanford Meisner wrote a lot about real listening and how it is not you listening *as the character* but rather *you* listening and reacting as you. One of Meisner's exercise principles was, *don't do anything unless something happens to make you do it … what you do doesn't depend on you; it depends on the other fellow* (Longwell, 1987).

Listening may be interpreted as having curiosity and exploration. If you are genuinely curious and want to discover what the other person is intending behind their words then you have an active, dynamic, functioning purpose. It will keep you in the scene much more than simply hearing and responding to words.

The freedom to look away from the camera does not mean you should hide yourself from it, though. Sometimes the character may look away because they are ashamed or are hiding something, but you must never look away from the camera because you, the actor, are feeling self-conscious. If you are truly listening, thinking, remembering and feeling then your eyes will go where they are supposed to. There are, of course, technical considerations and your inner actor may have to raise your head up slightly but don't dwell on it. Find simple reasons to favour the camera and direct your head and eyes towards it, and don't look down the lens unless you are asked to do so. A possible solution may be to situate points of focus relevant to the scene, such as the respondent, next to or beyond the camera as the narrower the shot, the closer to the lens your eye line must be. Otherwise we may not be able to see what is going on inside.

EXERCISE

Watch the online video at https://vimeo.com/251793757 and notice the difference between when the actor is truly listening and having an opinion on what is being said and when they are not.

14

NERVES AND NERVOUSNESS

What are nerves? Could it actually be excitement?

Being nervous can make you anxious, uneasy, apprehensive, edgy and worried. Clearly not a good situation for an actor to be in at the best of times, let alone when you are expected to perform in front of other people. Being nervous is the chief reason given for failure at auditions and can later manifest itself as stage fright once you have the job.

Imagine that you are at an audition or on set about to shoot your breakthrough scene with the star of the show. Everyone is watching and expecting you to make their job easier by being perfect. This is your make or break opportunity for the big time and your Oscar nomination, and the culmination of years of training and working on unpaid student films. If they like you they will hire you again; if they don't, your career is over. Suddenly your hands begin to sweat and tremble and your mouth dries as your nerves take hold, and your mind and body waver between jelly and blind panic. A space is created for your Impostor Syndrome, saboteur and limiting beliefs to enter and they begin to furiously jump up and down, all vying for attention. Ugh!

Most actors get nervous but some are more prone to nerves than others. How severe are your nerves and how can you prevent them from reaching the status of anxiety disorder? How can you maintain the necessary states for relaxation, creativity and spontaneity?

The physiological symptoms of nerves are partly caused by the brain sending messages down your nervous system to the parts of the body which are affected by them. These messages then impact on your body, increasing your heart rate, making your palms sweat, your breath speed up and your mouth dry, and hormones such as adrenaline are released into the bloodstream. Quite often though, this anxiety can be helpful. If you are being chased by a tiger or are jumping out of a plane, a burst of adrenaline becomes your best friend.

However, avoidable nerves in a non-fight or flight situation can become your worst enemy. They can cripple you with an anxiety from which you cannot escape, feeding on itself and making you more and more tense. Of course, some people may have major clinical anxiety problems but I'm not talking about that. I'm talking about the variety which does not need a prescription cure.

So, how can you deal with them immediately and simply?

A change of perspective and use of language helps. For example, the above physiological characteristics of nervousness are very similar to those of excitement. Your hands sweat, your body trembles and your heart rate increases. Here the words become exhilaration, enthusiasm, elation, expectation, adventure and passion. Earlier, I talked about the use of language and how changing the words you use can change your way of seeing the world and your mood. Neuro Linguistic Programming (NLP) is an industry based around this principle. So, when you begin to feel nervous, instead of saying *I'm nervous*, say *I'm excited*. When approaching a potentially stressful situation see it in a positive way rather than a negative one. Obviously believing that it's excitement is better than faking it but sometimes, as the saying goes, *you've got to fake it till you make it*. And, once again, the more you practise something the more it becomes a habit.

Nerves can be caused by fear of the unknown, but in performance the unknown is what you should be striving for and not something you should be scared of. Exploring, discovering and uncovering with no knowledge of the future is what gives depth and colour to your performance. It is where you find new perspectives, ideas and experiences. In an audition situation, this is what distinguishes you from the other auditionees. View the unknown as a positive which may trigger some physiological changes. Accept this, dive in and make your work and life more fruitful.

In the section on neuroplasticity I talked about replacing negative thoughts and limiting beliefs with more useful positive ones. Not fighting them but replacing them. The same is true with nerves. Instead of *trying* not to be nervous just focus on the task in hand more fully. Notice that there is a change in your physiology and move onto something else. Don't engage with the nerves and the chatter. It is about controlling your nerves rather than them controlling you.

Easier said than done? Not really. If you have prepared and know your material inside out and your inner character is working for and with you, there is no space for your brain to be sending nervousness down to the rest of your body. Your broadband pipe is so full of character hopes, dreams, fears and opinions that the conscious nerves of the inner actor get drowned out.

As a scene is an event in the middle of life there is no start or end point for your nerves, either. You cannot begin to feel nervous if you genuinely believe that you are already *in it* before the camera rolls. Concentrating on what is going on, focusing on the place in which the event is happening, your relationship and attitude towards the other characters and what you want from the scene are all that is useful and matters. Your 20 per cent inner actor may feel nerves, but they will be overcome and subsumed by the life of the 80 per cent inner character.

Let's say you are playing a character who has been in prison and you are about to see your partner for the first time in ten years. If you have done your prep work on your time inside thinking about how you miss them and have worked on your journey and thoughts leading up to you ringing their door bell, any nerves, impulses or emotions will be the character's, not yours. You will stop being an actor preparing for a scene and the nerves will not be yours but theirs.

The crew are watching you because it is their job, and this may cause consternation if you let it. If you think everyone is staring and wanting you to fail so they can laugh and call you an over-paid prima donna, or that they want you to get a move on because lunch is being served, realize that this is not the case. They are concerned about their own sphere of influence. Their own necks are on the line and they may be feeling nervous for their own reasons. They will be checking the lighting, the sound, the dolly and everything else that is nothing to do with you. Just focus on your job and what you are doing and all will be well.

And breathe, of course. There are plenty of breathing and meditation courses out there and it will serve you well to find one that suits you if you need one. However, focusing on your character is more beneficial than a half hour relaxation exercise as you will have to get to the character after your prep anyway. It is possible that you may forget that you are nervous once you are in the mind, body and soul of your character.

15
LINES AND LEARNING THEM

Learning lines can be straightforward and stress-free. If you let it.

That was amazing; how did you learn all those words? This often-asked question sums up many the layperson's knowledge of what an actor does to prepare for a role. There are loads of words and you must remember them all in the right order at the right time.

As we know, and as we have explored so far in this book, acting is about so much more than just learning lines. However, your inner actor must do their job and, as many drama teachers around the world will say, learn your darned lines.

Line learning is a necessity and an essential skill. The director will be very unimpressed if you don't do it. I worked on a film in New York and on the first day the other actor in my scenes asked for the size of the shot so he could put his script out of sight on the counter top. He hadn't learned his lines and was fired on the spot.

Fear of not knowing lines can increase the chatter of your saboteur, unbalance the inner actor/character mix and feed on the downward spiral of nerves. So, how can you ensure that your lines do not make you tense and stressed? There are countless theories and methods, some of which are listed below, but I want to focus on taking the pressure off and making it as simple for yourself as possible.

I have an unproven theory that learning lines is like taking a photograph – a permanent memory – using the old original camera obscura and daguerreotype cameras. You know the ones; the big boxes on a tripod with the lens at the front and sometimes a curtain at the back from under which the photographer observes the chosen image.

Taking a picture with these early cameras entailed removing the lens cap to let the light in, thereby exposing and projecting the image onto the light-sensitive chemical on the back plate. The plate was then removed and developed, resulting in a permanent photographic image.

My theory goes that you need only look at a page of script very carefully once or twice and it becomes imprinted on your mind. Like a photograph, the image passes through your eyes (the lens) and becomes permanently logged in your mind (the plate). You then spend your time reading it over and over to prove to yourself that all is present and correct (developing it) and settle it into your memory banks. It helps if a script is well written as you do not have to work too hard to make sense of it, but the general principle holds either way. You may just have to read it more times if it is poor.

I am not saying that you should only look at your script once and then sit back and relax. You need to put in the hours to ensure and confirm that you have learned it word for word before you put it aside and leave yourself alone. Go through the process slowly to give yourself a better chance. Allow the inner actor to do the work and store the information which will be retrieved by the inner character later. The point is that if you recognize it as a process you can learn lines in a more relaxed frame of mind. Which must be good.

It is interesting that sometimes you remember all your lines perfectly, running through them in your head as you walk along, yet at other times you can't remember them for the life of you. The words are clearly there but you just don't have access to them at that particular moment. Something is obviously standing in your way, which may be nerves or being distracted by something else. Breathe, find a peaceful space in your mind, trust that you know them and let the words come.

How many times do you have to read them before you believe that you have learnt and can recall them? A dozen? Fifty? A hundred? A thousand? My guess is not as many as you think. If the text is difficult, containing uncommon or unusual words, then it may take you a little longer, but it still begs the question as to how many times is enough? In my classes I ask the actors to look me in the eye and say *I know my lines*. When they believe it themselves, it is remarkable how the words come out exactly as written, even when they previously doubted themselves. There is a strong connection between use of language and behaviour. If you say you are happy enough times you will end up being happy, and if you say you are miserable enough times you will be miserable. If you say you know your lines then you know your lines. Once again, as Henry Ford said, *if you think you can, or you think you can't, you are right*. If you say you know your lines you do, whereas if you say you don't, you don't. Your brain believes you when you inform it that something is true.

The more you practise the easier it gets, of course, so read and learn lots of scripts. Learn monologues and dialogue and speak it out aloud. Practise as if you are preparing for a role or an audition. If you do this week after week you may be pleasantly surprised at how quickly it becomes easy. If you don't practise something and leave it until you need it, then don't be surprised when you can't use it.

This is especially true for those of you who are over 50 and think you have problems learning lines because of your age. Create new connections in your brain by going back to basics. Stimulate your brain and practise, practise, practise. Reawaken your old neural pathways and cut back the overgrown trails. Challenge yourself by remembering vehicle licence plate numbers having looked at them briefly as they speed past. You'll be surprised at how simple it is.

There are clearly words and phrases which you will find difficult to get your mouth around so practise them until they become second nature. If you have a difficult medical term, such as otorhinolaryngologist – ear, nose and throat scientist – for instance, break the word down, say it fifty times until it flows off your tongue then love the fact that you know what it means and how to pronounce it.

If you know you have difficulty with an imminent specific line and are consciously waiting for it, you will more than likely prove your saboteur right and mess it up by drawing attention to your inadequacies and living up to them. Stay in the moment with your character thoughts and you will not have space in your mind to worry about limiting and unnecessary babble.

There is a reason why you always stumble on the same word or phrase. It could be that you are not fully connected with what you are saying. Spend time working out exactly what you're talking about and how it connects with what comes after. Say to yourself that you love the line and you know it.

Thinking about your next line in advance is fatal. We sometimes do it in real life when we are not really listening to what the other person is saying and your characters may very well do the same, but if it is your inner actor preparing themselves, you are lost. Your inner character cannot give full attention to what is going on in front of you if your inner actor is focusing somewhere else.

Unless you are working as an elevator operator in a department store, when communicating with others you can't be sure of exactly where you are going next, what you are going to say and how you are going to say it. You must consider what others are saying or doing before you can react. Even the most self-absorbed people are impacted by what is around them; if you are on the Titanic waxing lyrical about your favourite shirt and the ship hits an iceberg, it is likely that you are going to speak your lines in a completely different way than if you were at a dinner party in your country home.

One of the easiest, most damaging, yet avoidable pitfalls when learning lines is saying them over and over in the same way, with the same inflections, volume and tone. The resulting rut this creates puts you in a pattern from which you cannot naturally deviate. You get stuck and say the line in the exact same way regardless of what you or the other characters are doing or feeling. Spontaneity becomes impossible if you are straitjacketed into a routine. The likelihood is that any deviation from exactly what you expected will cause your inner actor to panic and become tense.

Learn your lines like data in a monotone robotic pattern with either no inflections or a variance every time you repeat them. Sing them to the tune of different songs. Recite them with different rhythms and rises and falls on different words or parts of words. Break it up, learn it as data only and allow it to be delivered in the moment in the most suitable way for that particular interaction at that time. If you plan to say your line in a certain way and the other character has delivered theirs in a way that will make yours totally inappropriate, not only will you drop out of the scene, but the viewer will too. The inner actor must learn the lines in a neutral form and place them in the storage area of your brain, to be smoothly accessed and coloured by what the character needs in the moment.

If you believe what you are saying, there is no wrong way to say it. The director may ask you to emphasize a particular word in a particular way because he has a need for this scene to fit in with the arc of the film, but that is different. In these cases, it is still your responsibility to find the truth within the director's requirements and keep yourself real and believable.

Similarly, some directors like to give line readings without an explanation as to why you should speak in a certain way or what the change in meaning is. This can lead you to over-analyse and judge whether you are hitting the exact tone they require even though it is a non-scientific or precise amount. The result may easily be that your inner actor overwhelms your inner character, causing you, once again, to drop out of the scene.

Watch the great actors and notice how they breathe life into their lines. Meryl Streep puts a different emphasis on each word whilst maintaining the truth and meaning. Look for light and shade within the dialogue and use it as a clue to what is going on rather than a way to say something. Look for nuance. Playing the text literally is not necessarily what the writer intended. The lines ride on top of what is actually going on underneath. The script may say *I love you* but what is really going on below is *I hate you*. Sanford Meisner used the metaphor: *The text is like a canoe, and the river on which it sits is the emotion. The text floats on the river. If the water of the river is turbulent, the words will come out like a canoe on a rough river. It all depends on the flow of the river which is your emotion* (Longwell, 1987).

Unless you believe what you are saying and really live and breathe it, there is a risk that you will merely speak your lines in an interesting way; interesting but not connected. Do not artificially colour the text. The intention and strength of thought will colour the words so you don't have to add anything to show us what and how you are thinking. Again, it comes down to trusting that you and your preparation are enough and letting go of the result. At least the inner actor must. The inner character may be extremely aware of how they sound.

Stella Adler stated that you need to experience the lines before you can learn them. Once you understand what they mean it will be easier to learn: *The words come only after seeing. That's why it never helps to study the words or to memorize. You risk killing the ideas and the objects you're dealing with* (Adler, 2000).

The potential limitations of actioning

Actioning is the act of assigning an action or intention to each line in a script. On a certain line, you feel happy/sad/angry so should laugh/cry/shout. But how can you plan what your reaction is going to be if you don't yet know what the other actor will do? Surely their opinion should impact your response. Very few people remain exactly the same throughout their life or even in a moment. They change and so do their motivations, objectives, actions and reactions which are a response to something else happening. This change is what gives life. Other things make you react and the reaction will be different, at last slightly, every time. This spontaneous, broad and unpredictable palette is great for screen acting and directorial and editorial choice, and it helps create a rich and living production as a result.

Actioning is a useful tool when investigating possible reactions and intentions but leave this work behind in the rehearsal, whether you have been working alone or with other cast members. Put it aside, with the knowledge and trust that it is lodged in your filing cabinet, not inked into your script to rigidly play come what may. What may work once in rehearsal may not feel right in production. Actioning and making notes in the margin which tell you how to think or be in a specific moment will take you out of the scene. When the moment arrives in real time you may not actually be feeling the way you thought you would when you were preparing in your bedroom the night before. The other character may do something completely off the wall or out of left field. If you have planned your actions to stick to, the scene will collapse.

Everything you do is being done to something or someone and this is what provides the drive, momentum, direction and motivation of a scene. I kiss you to make my wife jealous; I look for the money in your wallet to show you that I don't trust you; I tell the police that you are guilty because I hate you. The character is affected by what they are receiving, which then affects what they do, and so on as the momentum builds with each *transaction*.

Playing actions can restrict this momentum and take you a step away from the character and what is going on in their mind in the moment. Generally, in life, you don't consciously focus on everything you are doing you just do it. When you eat you do so mechanically and with purpose. The newness and spontaneity of a situation needs a blank canvas where you do not know what is going to happen next. Even when you plan what you are going to say to a partner you want to leave, their reaction must dictate how the conversation goes. If they say, *thank God, I was going to finish with you myself tomorrow*, you will feel and react differently than if they break down crying, pleading with you to stay.

But what happens when we have set blocking to follow, I hear you ask? Isn't that the same as planning what is going to happen? The answer is no, not really. There must be some structure otherwise the camera will miss your sterling work and the film will never get finished. There are technical necessities which you must find a reason to employ to be seen by the camera and fit in with director's vision. The getting-out-of-your-own-way process is simple; your inner actor must find a reason to move from one place to another and practise until it becomes subconscious and ingrained in your muscle memory. Practise opening and closing the cupboard on your line, or moving across the set to another room, then leave yourself alone and trust it will materialize as instructed every time. Your inner character will move spontaneously and unselfconsciously in the moment as opposed to saying to themselves, *I must go here now because I've been told to,* and drop out.

Playing stakes and consequences

Stakes means what is being risked in a scene and by how much. The importance of what is at stake provides force and energy to a scene. It is not enough to just use an active verb, such as *persuade* or *show* them, there need to be consequences for actions and, in many cases, these consequences should be enormous. Otherwise there is no drama or movement within the scene. What happens if you don't persuade them? What happens then? If you are telling your son that they should not have stolen a car, for example, it has much more energy if they will go to jail as a result or that you have to sell your house to pay the fine.

When you have more to lose you behave differently than when you have nothing. James Bond is always on the edge of high stakes and the way he responds is where the action happens. He bets the maximum with the result that those around him significantly change their behaviour.

But how can you play stakes? What is at stake may be your partner leaving you or going to jail, but how can you play that? You cannot play the result. Again, all you can do is prepare solidly and play your part to its fullest. Use the concept of stakes to help inform your perception of what happens in the script but don't get hung up on them or use them artificially.

Stakes have consequences and it is this which adds colour and power to the action. There are multiple consequences to an action which lead to several more, in the same way that we have multiple concurrent thoughts. Consequences can be one thing happening or another thing as well as being one thing happening and another. Hundreds of thoughts and consequences fly through your subconscious every time you make a decision and the permutations are limitless, only restricted by the amount of time you have to work on the part. By preparing a list of potential outcomes, the probability that your inner character will make real choices in the moment is strengthened.

Think about the consequences of possible immediate physical or vocal actions within the scene. In the *Kramer vs Kramer* restaurant scene I referred to earlier, Ted may be considering what would happen if he leant across the table and slapped Joanna. Will he get arrested? What happens if he does? Will his son be taken away from him? Will it wake Joanna up to what she is doing? Will he knock over her glass of wine and ruin her dress? What will everyone in the restaurant be thinking? Will the cops be called and will he lose his job? If he loses his job what then?

So, like actioning, stakes and consequences are useful tools with which you can explore the scene but they should be deposited in your subconscious not your conscious.

When rehearsing and exploring, work without the script in your hand as much as possible. If you are holding it as a backup, just in case, you will be tempted to direct your attention towards it in moments of doubt rather than totally focusing on what is going on and searching for the words in your head like we do as humans. The most interesting acting is usually not the smoothest and most perfect. In life, we forget where we are in a thought; we stumble and stutter and dry up in the middle of sentences. So why not in a scene if it is appropriate? The ebb and flow of speech is what makes it interesting. The variety of pitch and tone and speed helps create an impact and strength in what you are relaying. So, fear not the stumble and welcome the freedom which it brings.

Forgetting lines can produce some of the best and most truthful moments on film. Suddenly, your inner actor realizes that you have no idea what comes next; just like in real life. So, it reaches into your filing cabinet searching for your line in the script whilst picking up a feeling of fear or dread along the way. However, the viewer does not know that this is what is happening and all they see is a person deep in an emotional thought. By keeping calm and recognizing that this happens, switch over and allow your inner character to be the one who doesn't know what to say next. Let them search their own filing cabinet and come forward with the natural response.

Some ways people learn lines – a non-exhaustive list

- Learn them walking round the house, doing dishes or gardening.
- Learn them by rote like data – flat and uninterestingly.
- Vary different words each time you run the specific line.
- Sing them with a different tune each time.
- Go through one line at a time and go back to the beginning every time you make a mistake.

- Write them down.

- Copy them out again and again.

- Record and listen to them on headphones throughout the day.

- Record the other character's lines and answer them in your head.

- *Sometimes I re-type all my lines on an old typewriter to help me learn them. When I was younger, I would write out the entire part meticulously in longhand, four or five times over. It would make it feel as if I had written it myself. It was a way of belonging to the piece, I guess.* – Anthony Hopkins, who has also been quoted as saying …

- *… I learn lines by reading my script hundreds of times* (Hollywood Reporter, 2006).

- It is rumoured that Johnny Depp, Marlon Brando, Angela Lansbury and others have used an ear piece, with somebody reading their lines to them as they go.

- There are apps for learning lines.

EXERCISE

Pick your favourite film script and learn scenes from it. Learn it section by section page by page. Once you have finished, pick another script and do the same thing.

EXERCISE

The words ride on top of what is really going on. Choose ten different moods and film yourself saying the line *I love you and I want to move in with you* for each. Review and notice the difference between what you say and what you mean. See https://vimeo.com/251793902 for an example.

Once you have proven to yourself that you can remember lines, I give you permission to accept this as a truth.

16
ADJUSTING YOUR VOCAL LEVELS

Making yourself heard and understood is vital. But it's not rocket science.

Volume

Training your voice, developing your vocal technique, having a range of accents, learning to breathe to the end of the line and varying your cadences and tones will undoubtedly give you more opportunities for work. There are many teachers, classes and books written on the subject and it will be beneficial for you to invest in the training. However, overthinking and worrying about it can stand in your way.

Many stage actors, whether musical theatre or otherwise, fear that they will have issues with volume if they work with a camera. They are so used to projecting towards the back of the auditorium that they feel their performances will be too big. They obsess about it and forget they have instincts which manage the problem for them.

Although many actors are larger-than-life characters with interesting and varied personalities and ranges, they do not, or at least most of them do not, shout their way around life. If you are having an intimate conversation in a restaurant you automatically lower your voice to an appropriate volume. If you are shouting across the bar to order a drink you will also find that suitable level to pitch. You don't have a volume meter which indicates a necessary rise or fall in levels, you just do it.

Once you have worked with microphones, whether pinned to your clothing or hung above your head on a boom, your instincts and experience will take over and you will adjust your volume appropriately. In the same way, if the sound guy complains that your jewellery is hitting the table every time you gesticulate, rendering the sound unusable, you will learn very quickly to not do it again. As you will learn not to close a door or make any other noise over yours or someone else's line. In fact, you don't even have to wait to make a mistake on set, you can practise at home.

Working with a radio or lapel mic is clearly different than projecting on stage, but once again, a little experience and a lot of practice will teach you all you need to know. I learnt a huge lesson on how *not* to use a radio mic when I worked in Atlantic City once. And I use the word *once* advisedly. I was playing James Bond in a huge New Year's Eve extravaganza which involved dancers, pyrotechnics, $130,000 of lighting and the saving of the New Year clock. Important business.

It was assumed I knew what I was doing and that I knew how to use one of those radio mics which straps to your cheek or your forehead. In fact, I had never used one and had no idea about appropriate levels of projection and volume. Subsequently, at the technical rehearsal, a couple of hours before the show went up, I belted my song out beautifully and with gusto, blowing out my mic with the resulting unwelcomed silence. I blamed it on the equipment and when, during the performance in front of 800 of the hotel's most important clients, the same thing happened with their backup mic, I was convinced it was nothing to do with me. Consequently, I had to sing my songs and make my James Bond quips without any electronic help and the audience didn't hear a word of it. I later realized that you don't need to project when you're wearing a radio mic. Oops. In these circumstances, ensuring that the audience hears you is the job of the sound guy and he enables you to tell the story in an intimate way to a large room. Believe what you are doing and let them do the rest.

On-screen it is the same. You know that not shouting into a microphone makes sense, as anyone who has listened to their friends singing karaoke or people on the train *talking* into their phones will attest to. Tell the story, connect with the material and feel what you feel. He may ask you to tweak it a little, but let the sound guy adjust the volume.

You have instincts which have been built up by previous experience. Instincts allow actions to happen naturally, many of which don't require a training course if you trust yourself. Your instincts will naturally dictate your volume. Furthermore, belting out your feelings at top volume will more than likely disperse them into the ether rather than allow them to build and concentrate inside you (see the section on the pressure cooker).

Control of your breathing is as important as controlling your actions. If you don't take in enough oxygen to speak the full thought, then your speech won't sound like you or the writer intended. It will break the thought into smaller slices and change the route of travel. The procedure is that you have a thought in a nano-second, the brain searches for the appropriate words and sentences, then fulfils this thought by speaking. If you unnaturally disrupt this process because you don't have enough air in your lungs, then you limit the chance for your character to get what they want. Additionally, if your thought changes mid-sentence there may not be enough flexibility within your breath to effect this change.

Of course, the character may not have enough breath and may be forced onto weird spacing and fragmentation of patterns. The sight of a beautiful location may take their breath away or a tiger jumping out of the bushes likewise, but that is different. Your job is to serve the character and their life not the other way around.

Practise, practise, practise to the point where it becomes a habit and you are not falling into the fatal trap of working on technique in the middle of a scene. Consciously deciding in the moment when to breathe will take you out the scene, or restrict your options in relation to what you are receiving from the other actors.

Speed

Another all too frequent issue is talking too quickly and not leaving enough space for the scene to breathe or for you to feel the truth within it. Maybe there is a hangover from the theatre where the director shouts *you can drive a bus through that gap, hurry up*? However, on film, if you talk too rapidly or reply to the other character too quickly, you don't give yourself enough chance for the circumstances to have an impact on you, them or the viewer. It will not allow a barbed vocal dagger to land or a statement of love to hit home, as you have moved on too quickly to the next thought.

Many actors speed along with their dialogue because they haven't connected with the material. Their brain wants to get it over with as quickly as possible because it does not associate with what is happening, resulting in an unintelligible and disconnected torrent of words.

So, SLOW DOWN. There is a lot more time than you often allow yourself. Watch your favourite programs and notice that most of them don't constantly and hurriedly talk back and forth – unless it's *The West Wing* (Sorkin, 1999–2006), of course. There is space for the character to think and react allowing both yourself and the viewer the freedom and opportunity to feel the emotion behind what is being said. It is like a snowball that picks up snow as it goes, but less so if it is rolling too quickly.

If the director wants the scene to be quicker that is different, but nine times out of ten it is usually the pace of the scene they want to speed up not your delivery. They can also play with the speed and take out any spaces they don't need in the edit.

The same speed issue is often also true in auditions. There is a tendency to rush in, rush your scene and then rush out so as to not waste the casting director's time. Watch auditions on YouTube and notice how the successful ones are generally more considered and even paced. It is your time so take your time.

EXERCISE

Carry on your daily chores while speaking a monologue, taking care not to speak over any sounds you may make. You will get in the habit of not making the noises at all or of spacing your dialogue to accommodate them.

EXERCISE

Talk to your lapel or collar. Recite a monologue or just read the newspaper. Notice how much more connected and internal you feel, whilst talking more quietly in the process.

EXERCISE

Rehearse by talking into a mobile phone. This should make it more intimate and quieter without losing the emotion of what is going on.

EXERCISE

Standing directly in front of, and talking straight into the camera – or to a mark on the side of the lens – recount what you did yesterday afternoon. As you are speaking, walk slowly away as far you can.

Review and notice how your volume instinctively and naturally got louder the further away from the camera you went. Trust your instincts.
See https://vimeo.com/251794174 for an example.

17
SIZE MATTERS

Too big? If you connect with the material, follow your instincts and use your common sense, the size of your performance will generally take care of itself.

Less is more

And so, we enter the realm of less is more, which is one of the most frustrating and annoying statements espoused in our industry. Less what? More what? Less humanity? More humanity? More thinking? Less passion? Less movement? What? No one has given me an adequate answer to this question. I have had directors who have said to me, you know, less, just less. But what do they mean? Do less to achieve more? Maybe add less than do less? Do they mean smaller, and if so, how small? Miniscule? Non-existent? Do they mean less expressive? Less obvious? Less happy? Less fat?

Very frequently the answer will be more internal but if you have prepared correctly isn't that what you are doing in any case? If you are already internalizing, then how can you do that any more than you are already doing?

Many acting classes proclaim that the actor should be as still as possible or, even better, not move at all. They state that not moving your face is the major difference between stage and screen acting. They insist that your forehead creases and your eyebrows move too much, so don't do it. Do not move your head or you will never work in this industry. Well, why not just get Botox and remove the chances of your face moving altogether?

I don't want to watch two people not moving and rigidly talking to each other for an hour and a half and I'm not alone in liking characters with life and energy. Think of Jack Nicholson, Meryl Streep or Johnny Depp in almost every role they have ever played. They move and are fascinating and believable to watch. Robert De Niro creases his face a lot, and if you don't believe me watch *Analyze This* and *Analyze That!*

If your inner character is resonating, it is possible to maintain connected and real facial expressions. Don't allow your inner actor to stifle your inner character by thinking about how you are looking. Facial movements are fine unless they are a result of your inner actor not connecting enough with the material and pushing and indicating to cover it up. When you trust this and are free, you can change the levels of intensity of thinking in the moment and be expressive without it being too much. Restrictive instructions, such as do less with your face, will only serve to keep you out of the action not in it. Your brain will be focused on considerations outside the character's, such as how many creases are OK, or, is this exactly what the director wants?

Film is about life and in real life nobody is stock-still all the time unless they have an ailment. People move. Watch them move their eyebrows, scratch their heads, touch their noses, pull their sleeves down or throw their heads back and laugh. These behaviours shine a light on their inner life and can be intrinsic to the action.

A companion statement to *do* less is *stop* acting, but what does this mean? What is acting and why can it be a horrible word to actors and directors? Surely you are paid to act? Acting may sometimes mean not being real so I get where they could be coming from – for example, acting sad rather than being sad. Again, it is about terminology. Reframe and rephrase *stop* acting to *believe* what you are you saying, or any phrase which suits you better. Remove the desire to people-please by doing what you think the director wants and replace it with a thought through and realized truth in what you as the character feel. If the director is still unhappy then you can talk it through with them as an internal exploration of what the character thinks and feels.

Concerning yourself with being too big or small will get in your way. You have great instincts so trust them. Make the stakes big then feel the size of the shot. You will instinctively know that if you are shooting a wide shot you have more scope for movement than if you are shooting a close-up. If it is an extreme close-up you will instinctively know not to toss your head around as it will look huge on the screen. If you are unsure, then you must make it your responsibility to ask the shot size and adjust accordingly.

Many people rate Meryl Streep as one of the finest actors of our time. Having seen her in *The Seagull* in Central Park in New York with, amongst others, Philip Seymour Hoffman, Christopher Walken and Natalie Portman, I can attest to the fact that this is true. My most enduring memory of the show is of her cartwheeling onto stage. As she was playing a self-involved, self-absorbed show-off actress, it was a huge but totally appropriate move. Watch her on-screen performances, such as *August, Osage County* (Wells, 2013), and you will still see a very expressive, emotionally accessible yet technically excellent actress. She doesn't minimize her character and personality just because she's on-screen; she remains exciting, real and truthful. Her face moves, her eyebrows move, her forehead creases, she throws her head back in laughter. Do you find it distracting? I'll bet 90 per cent of you don't. People want to watch and are moved by her humanity in a way that they wouldn't if she wasn't human and real. What we care about most are her obstacles and how she overcomes them. In the film *The River Wild* there is a moment when she is talking to Kevin Bacon about her husband, whom Bacon's character has apparently just murdered, and she laughs. She is laughing in his face although she is devastated inside. She doesn't show him or us the devastation but it is there. She is not worrying about whether she was creasing her forehead.

If you really connect with the material and believe what you are saying and the shot is not an extreme close-up, whatever you do is pretty much appropriate. As Hamlet almost said to The Players, connect the moving eyebrow with the word and the word with the moving eyebrow. There was no indication in Hamlet's advice that they should keep as still as possible. Of course, this was in the days before screen acting but why should screen acting be any less interesting and emotionally engaging?

Superfluous movement, indicating and unconnected movements generally occur when you don't believe what you are saying and will often be inappropriate as they are not truthfully motivated. The key is to be real and believable and, if it is apposite, expressive. Some actors embellish and add expressions and gestures because they are afraid of being boring, but in these cases I challenge you to dare to be boring if that's what it is. Once again, don't fake it, feel it.

The shot size should not matter in your character preparation as it will not affect how real and believable you will be from moment to moment. You will still work on the truth of the situation and your relationships and opinions of others. You will still know where you are coming from and where you want to go.

There is little doubt that you will be employed to play a role based on your personality and what you bring to the part. If you are just a talking head with no expression then you have no chance. I'm guessing that you became an actor because you have an ability and desire to tell stories or play characters. The most interesting storytellers are those who have expression and draw us in with their connection and emotion. I once watched a lecture by an eminent scientist on a subject of great interest to me but I can't remember a word of what he said because he was so incredibly boring. He stood still behind a lectern with no passion or life. Your job is to tell the story but also to entertain.

Some parts require the actor to be still and that is fine if it is the character being still. Watch Al Pacino in the *Godfather* films. His character, Michael Corleone, is very high status and his stillness intensifies the threat he exudes. But watch it closely and you will see him moving. In the scene in the restaurant in *The Godfather* (Coppola, 1972) where he kills his first and second victims, the camera gradually moves in to a close-up of his face as he is preparing to do the deed. And his eyes are moving all over the place. His mouth is opening and closing. Did he not go to the class on effective screen acting?

Use these great actors as role models and show us your personality and interpretation of the material. After all, that is a major reason why we go to the cinema.

It would be remiss of me to dismiss the technical side, however, as this is as important as the above. There are plenty of great books out there which focus on this and you could do a lot worse than reading Bill Britten's *From Stage to Screen* (2015). There are lists of do's and don'ts on close-ups, such as not bringing your hands or props in and out of the frame and not swaying back and forth. Learn these rules then put them aside, out of your way.

EXERCISE

Watch all of your favourite actors in all of your favourite films and TV programmes and notice how much everyone moves!

PART FOUR

TOOLS TO LIVE SOMEONE ELSE'S LIFE

18

THE INNER ACTOR AND INNER CHARACTER

You are both the actor and the character. In preparation you are the actor, in performance the character. Be in charge of who, what and when.

Once you are out of your own way and have eased the pressure from yourself, how can you then begin the task of effectively moving towards someone else and playing other people? There is a process but do you become the character, does the character become you, are they a part of you or is it you plus extras? I have never fully understood the differences between these viewpoints and I am sure that it doesn't matter as much how you define it as what you do with it.

One of my clients stated that, *I'm never going to do just me*, and they are right, there is always something to add. Even actors like Michael Caine, who rarely stray too far from themselves, play people from different eras with different backgrounds and needs. They may not be immersive character actors, such as Philip Seymour Hoffman or Gary Oldman, but they still have to build characters.

But where do you start and how can you simplify it? In his *headstrong* approach to screen performance, Michael Ferguson identifies two delineated sides of the process, which he defines as the *inner artist* and *inner character* (I prefer to use the term *inner actor* rather than *artist* and will be referring to it this way from here on). Each side has a separate function in preparation and performance, allowing you to identify your responsibilities as an actor and separate them cleanly from the thoughts, behaviours and actions of the character. The clarity, connection and relationship between the two sides will then make your work more precise, manageable and repeatable.

You may equate this partition to the different sides of the brain; the inner actor being the analytical, logical and objective left brain which does much of the grunt work, and the inner character as the intuitive, creative, subjective right brain which is spontaneous and free to experiment in the moment.

The inner actor instigates the creation of the character, reads the script and begins to make judgements and assessments. They ask who, what, where, when, why and how and pull together a portfolio of what they need to find out before the character is ready to be introduced. Like Dr Frankenstein finding the component parts and preparing his monster before he switches on the power. They ensure that you do your research, learn your lines and blocking, get to the set without tripping on the cables, stand on your mark at the correct angle and all the other necessary and important functions needed before your character engages with the action. Once the inner character starts working and takes over, the inner actor then steps back and becomes the curator, keeping an eye on what is going on but not interfering with or judging the creative process.

The inner character *is* the character. It is the creative side. Having worked on their history, relationships, needs and desires and what makes them tick, if you trust yourself and your preparation and get out of the character's way, this inner character takes over and becomes you. Or you become them whichever way round you want to see it. Although it is *your* brain thinking the thoughts and *your* body and soul having the impulses and feeling the emotions, you begin to experience them as the characters' through their filters.

Preparation is key and the more you prepare, the deeper and broader the results will become. Having a range of options from which your character can consciously and subconsciously choose will give more spontaneous in-the-moment opportunities. If you prepare yourself well, and your inner actor has accumulated and stored a catalogue of potential thoughts and behaviours, you will be able to re-take the scene over and again with freshness and truth as your character will not, and cannot, predict exactly what their future will bring. If your character has the option of deciding whether to stay or go and in peace or with hate, the unfolding of the scene itself will present the answer in the moment.

At the same time, the more you cram your brain with character thoughts, the less space there is for the inner actor to come along and over-think things when it is not their time to do so. If you are so involved with what the character wants and is doing you can't be noticing the crew watching and judging you, what time lunch is or whether the director will like you enough to give you another job after this one. You will not judge how you say a line and you will not drop out.

There is a time and a place for each side to be at the fore, which begs the question as to the percentage balance or split between them and how much you can or should strive for.

In preparation, the inner actor has a higher percentage as they are doing most of the work. As your preparation takes shape and form and you are confidently settled with who you are playing/becoming and showtime is approaching, the inner character's percentage increases exponentially until it is dominant.

However, 100 per cent inner character is not only unreasonable and unachievable, it is also undesirable. On the set, your inner actor is still an important and necessary component and your brain needs it to be functioning. But not excessively. Too much inner actor is detrimental to your connection with your character's and scene partner's lives. It is not emotionally invested in the script and the space which is created away from the character may allow your saboteur to start judging and commenting, and consequently take you out of the scene. An *about right* level (maybe 80 per cent inner character, 20 per cent inner actor, or so) will allow you to block out anything unrelated. If you are in a cold West London studio acting in a scene set in twelfth-century Africa you cannot allow yourself to be distracted by the crew, the camera or the real temperature. Keeping close to your part in the world of the film and the given circumstances will stand you in good stead. The camera will become just another piece of the furniture. The inner actor knows it is there and ensures you relate to it but 80 per cent of you will ignore its existence. Later chapters will offer you tools to help with this.

Daniel Day-Lewis is recognized as being one of the most committed, dedicated and immersive character actors but even he is not totally 100 per cent inner character. He must still exist in the here and now on some level, whether to relax, conserve energy or to stop wanting to kill people if that is the role he is playing. When he was working on *Gangs of New York* he stayed in character on set as Bill the Butcher. However, British actor Stephen Graham tells of how he was sitting with Day-Lewis one day waiting to shoot and, although he was totally in costume and in character, he began talking to Graham about football. It must have been strange, Bill the Butcher talking about his favourite football team, Millwall.

The inner actor is a vital chunk of your self-preservation. The nature of drama is that many of the players have problems and idiosyncrasies which are not appropriate for our society. You will play depressed people, addicts, killers and sexual predators. If you are playing a psychotic who wants to murder every person they see, you cannot, should not and must not take these thoughts out into the world and action them. This is clearly not only illegal and wrong but also not what acting is about. Your inner actor shuts this psycho down when you need to. If you are lining up at the catering truck and they have run out of your favourite vegetables you must not scream at, belittle or kill the chef if that is what your character would do. You must switch off. Thank god for your inner actor is what I say!

I am often asked how to prevent from being stuck in the character and going crazy if you live so deeply in it. How do you close the door? Well, that's why you need your inner actor; to help find and employ your own technique to switch it off. Some people have a shower when they finish working on a character and wash them away, others go for a run or walk through an imaginary cleansing area. Most of the time I am sure you will just switch it off by finishing the shoot but a conscious technique to move on is a good safeguard.

Unless you're hypnotized (not recommended on a movie set), it is nigh on impossible – and unnecessary – to totally cut yourself from the world around you. A high enough inner actor/character percentage split is sufficient (around 80/20). You know the feeling when you are *in the zone*, when nothing else exists apart from the scene or the event which is taking place? You get to the end of the conversation and can't remember if you delivered all your lines or not? When the director says, *I really liked it when you scratched your nose, do it again*, and you can't remember scratching your nose at all so must check with the continuity person? This is when your inner character is resonating, vibrating and firing on all cylinders. That high point of satisfaction when you have lived and breathed life into all your preparation. When you forget that you are an actor in performance and genuinely and completely feel the anxiety, pain or total bliss which the script dictates your character must feel.

To strengthen the connection further in rehearsal and on set, use *I statements* and relate to your character in the first person. It is after all *you* who is thinking and doing, and you don't have to *get into character* if you are already believing that you *are* the character. It is *I* think this, *I* will go over there and *I* will pick up the pen rather than *he* is upset and *he* walks over to the door.

Stanislavski talked about the *magic if*. As *if* you are nervously hiding in an attic from the police, as *if* you are in love with a complete bastard, as *if* you are standing at your parent's grave. But it is always *you*. Or *me* or *I*, if you see what I mean?

As an artist, which is what you are, immerse yourself in the imagined reality of the script. Dive in, feel it wash around you and enjoy the experience. The deeper you go, the more your inner character has to work with and the more creative and impulsive you can be. Meisner put it well: *The foundation of acting is the reality of doing. If you are really doing it, then you don't have time to watch yourself doing it. You only have the time and energy to do it* (Longwell, 1987).

EXERCISE

Russell Crowe talks about filling and appropriating himself with the *character's information* resulting in subtle specific attitudes and actions arising naturally. The detailed, but not exhaustive, list of character information in Appendix 5 will give you a good start with your character preparation. Work through it with any character of your choice, use your imagination and feel free to make it all up. You may want to use a character from *Friends and Crocodiles,* such as Paul or Lizzie in the scene below. Use people, places and things from your own life, such as your real dog, sister, choice of newspaper or food preference. There is no right and wrong and you may go back and change your answers. If you want to change the information from the United Kingdom to the United States and bring period pieces into the twentieth century, feel free. Have fun and don't worry about making it perfect. As you now know, there is no such thing!

Concentrate fully, write it out and absorb the information into your body and mind. Then put your notes aside, trust your subconscious and, with a partner, try it out. If you are not currently working on a script, play the scene below from *Friends and Crocodiles*. Let it affect you. You will not be thinking about your dog's name in the middle of the scene but it will allow you to trust who you are and give you a foundation and breadth in which the character lives.

Once you have used the full list a few times you will know which questions work for you and those you don't need to consider, and take appropriate short cuts.

INT. THE HOUSE. THE LANDING. NIGHT

LIZZIE is sitting in the window seat on the 1st floor landing, as all the surreptitious scurrying is going on. PAUL suddenly appears in front of her. He looks pale and shocked. It is the first time we have ever seen him angry.

PAUL: Are you crazy … ?

LIZZIE: Am *I* crazy?

PAUL: WHAT HAVE YOU DONE … ?! You can't call the police.

LIZZIE: I have called the police.

PAUL: You've gone mad … You realize who's here … ?! Do you know who some of the guests are?

LIZZIE: Somebody was going to get hurt. I couldn't find you. I had to do something –

PAUL: That's a lie, Lizzie … That's not the real reason –

LIZZIE suddenly erupts.

LIZZIE: Not the real reason?! … I see … And what is the real reason … ?! WHAT IS THE REAL REASON? – TELL ME!

PAUL: The real reason … You want something I can't give you … And you can't forgive me for that … It's not my fault, I can't, I don't –

He stares at her lovely red dress. LIZZIE suddenly realises he thinks she put it on for him.

LIZZIE: Go on – say it … SAY IT, PAUL! (*Staring at him; she is incandescent.*) You really think this is about sex?! … You arrogant shit … It doesn't occur to

you for one single moment does it – that not everybody finds you irresistible
… (*She stares coldly at him.*) There was a fire. There was dangerous behaviour
… There were children at this party … People were going to get really badly
hurt. Somebody had to take control … So I called the police. And I suggest you
go downstairs and talk to them. Explain away your party …

PAUL stares at her. LIZZIE meets his look.

LIZZIE: Don't worry – I'm already leaving. You will never see me again.

EXERCISE

Another way of quickly getting to the core of a character and producing full
character breakdowns is with the use of astrological signs of the zodiac.
Look up star signs and whether they are shy, introvert, extrovert, duplicitous
or kind. For example, an Aquarian character can be an independent, kind,
fun, rebellious, progressive thinking, stubborn, sarcastic, aloof and an
intellectual visionary. Whereas a Capricorn may be responsible, patient,
ambitious, resourceful, loyal, dictatorial, inhibited, conceited, distrusting and
unimaginative.

Choose one for Paul or Lizzie. Fill in the character traits consistent with that
sign.

19

TRUTH: IT ALL STARTS WITH YOU (AND A LITTLE ABOUT METHOD ACTING)

The word truth means 'fact' and 'things that are real'. Finding the truth within your acting will make it real for yourself and the viewer.

To keep our audiences engaged and to move them, we need them to be invested in the story. As in life, they can mostly tell whether someone is being honest or not and whether they are genuinely angry, sad or merely faking. If they sense that the actors – as opposed to the characters – are not being truthful and are pretending, then they will not believe or invest in them.

It is often stated that acting is pretending to be someone else. But it isn't. Acting is not about pretending to do something or be someone. You're not going to move anyone by pretending. You can't effectively pretend to laugh, cry or feel any true emotion, in the same way that you can't pretend to walk or pick up a cup of coffee. Your 80 per cent inner character is not pretending and must truly live as opposed to pretend to live. If you don't believe what is happening, how can the viewer?

You *are* that lawyer from Illinois, that socialite from New York, that policeman from London. You are the one feeling, thinking, talking and moving. It is not someone else, it is you. It's you walking down the street, interacting with the bus driver, being shouted at by your scene partner. You take on the characteristics of those you are playing but it is you at the core.

One of the reasons people respond so favourably to actors such as Robert De Niro, Al Pacino and Meryl Streep is that they engage with and adopt the truth of their characters and their, often harsh, circumstances. Through this truth they provide moments of spontaneity which surprise and thrill us. It is as if they *are* those people stuck in tricky situations from which they don't know how to escape.

Actors must help the viewer suspend disbelief and commit to the story. In the film *The Theory of Everything* (Marsh, 2014), you know you are watching an actor, not Stephen Hawking. Eddie Redmayne doesn't move you because he is pretending to be Stephen Hawking but because you really believe he is going through his experiences. Redmayne probably read the script a load of times, explored and experienced the life of the character and then put the work aside, after which he simply talked and listened to the people whom he came into contact with. He genuinely and truthfully reacted in the way he was feeling at that time based on the history and experiences he had given himself. He truthfully behaved like his version of Stephen Hawking would in those given circumstances.

In life, most of us don't walk around consciously thinking about who we are, what we are doing and where we come from. We just exist with all our experiences and emotions packed together. You live through your innate and learnt instincts. You look at your watch without thinking *I must look at my watch now to see what the time is.* You just do it. Pretence and conscious self-reflection does not help you build and maintain an emotional journey. More than likely it will have the opposite impact. You may feel that you are helping the viewer easily identify that you need to know the time by pretending to look at your watch, but if it is not truthful your brain will ask what on earth you're doing? So, your brain drops out and you have to work harder to get back in. You need to believe that what you are doing is real so that you can forget about it. Practise as if you actually see the watch and time. Work on why this particular time is of significance and make it truthful to yourself and us for when the camera is rolling. That way, there will be a real, solid and unconscious impact and response to your actions.

I remember the first time I saw someone use a tear stick on a set. It was an emotionally charged scene set at a wake where my daughter was being grieved over. A few of the cast had been sitting round laughing and joking until the assistant director called us to the set. They then dabbed what looked like a chap stick under their eyes and tears began to trickle down their cheeks. It seemed an interesting and easy way of getting to where their characters needed to be but when I saw the scene on the big screen it was obvious to me that they were faking. You could see who was really feeling and experiencing the emotional reasons for their tears and those who had painted it on.

Of course, it depends upon whether you want to be an authentic actor who works hard on your craft and does justice to the piece, or someone who just wants to look good. But the more you feel it, the more you can manipulate it by holding back from going full throttle; and the more the viewer will feel it and understand the human condition and broaden the scope of their own lives. Take people on a journey and invest *them* in it, as if you are in a documentary as a real person telling real stories, being truthful and using yourself as the starting point. Sanford Meisner calls it *living truthfully under imaginary circumstances*, which about sums it up.

A film is not about the words nor is it about the actors consciously displaying their feelings towards a camera. The film *Blue Valentine* (Cianfrance, 2010) was largely improvised and the camera acted as witness to the relationship between the two main characters. For the scene where they were walking across the Manhattan Bridge, the director Derek Cianfrance told Ryan Gosling that Michelle Williams had a secret and that he had to do whatever he could to get that secret out of her. He directed Williams to do whatever she could to keep it from him. They shot for about an hour with Gosling repeating the lines, *Tell me what's wrong? Tell me what's wrong?* She wouldn't tell him until finally he climbed over the fence of the bridge with no safety net. Thankfully, Williams stopped him and told him enough to bring him down. Who knows what would have happened if she hadn't. The truth within the situation and the belief of the actors is what moves and shakes us, and the scene was made more powerful as a result.

Be wary, also, of going to an acting technique too soon. Read the script over and over and allow it to start working on you. The material will start to connect with you personally, emotionally and physically and you will get a fuller understanding of what it all means. Finding a pinprick-sized spark of truth within your core which then, as you continue to read, spreads out to become belief and conviction. I equate it with how life starts: the fertilization of an idea which grows and spreads to form a larger, more complex organism. You recognize that the truth of the scene or event or slice of life or interaction, or whatever you want to call it, starts with you. If you really believe it then it's not fake and nor are you. As Stella Adler may have said, *if you believe it, it's true*. Once you reach this point you can then layer on character attributes, thoughts and consequences.

For those of you who are interested in a philosophical approach to life, you can't get closer to the truth than you can through acting as it gets to the heart of human interaction. You dissect your characters and find out what they really want, think and feel and then explore yourself to find in you what is necessary to adequately portray them for the benefit of others.

If you believe that what you have worked on is true, then you will relax more easily into the character and believe that the experiences you have created for them are real. In the same way that a nightmare sticks with you for the rest of the day because you believe you experienced the events.

Method acting

The words *Method acting* are probably the most misrepresented and misused combination of words in our profession. Any time anyone stays in character or shouts, they are called a Method actor. Any time anyone has done research or worked out what the character had for breakfast they are similarly painted with what is perceived to be a negative and dirty brush. While many actors adopt this approach on top of the Method technique – and why not – this is not what Method acting actually is.

Method acting is a training technique which uses your own personal experiences to find the truth to get closer to and inform those of your character. It explores your psyche and allows true and honest expression so that the viewer will feel what you truthfully feel.

The Method was developed in New York by Lee Strasberg in the first half of the twentieth century. He had observed productions by the theatre actor, director and founder of modern acting Konstantin Stanislavski and his touring Moscow Arts Theatre, and was struck by the absolute truth and reality of what he saw on stage. The theatrical style prior to this time was very much representational with actors indicating their feelings and actions; when you are happy or sad you behave in this way or that. Stanislavski and his *system* focused on acting as experiencing rather than representing, and feeling rather than showing.

Along with Stella Adler, Sanford Meisner and others from the Group Theatre in New York City, he set out to explore the personal and emotional identification of characters and acting.

Much has been written about Lee Strasberg's Method, some of it complimentary, some of it otherwise, but for me it is a useful technique to add to the tools which you will learn elsewhere. It is also an addition to, not a replacement for, your talent and should not be used in a take unless you cannot access what you need without it.

I see the method as divided into three sections:

1. Sense memory. I will cover it more fully in the next chapter but, in essence, sense memory is the retrieval and re-creation of past situations, feelings, physical states, people, places and events through the use of your senses, to help find and bind the truth in your present performance.

2. Affective memory. This uses the retrieval and re-creation of real, powerful and emotional stored memories to underpin and support a truthful moment in a scene; hence its pseudonym, *emotional recall* – see the earlier chapter on emotions. Its use should primarily be in preparation for a scene or when you are uninspired during one and need a *result*.

3. Substitution/character work. This helps you use other people and/or animals to create the physicality, vocal content and inner life of your characters. Just as Johnny Depp is rumoured to have used Keith Richards from the Rolling Stones as the base for his Captain Sparrow in the *Pirates of the Caribbean* films, you can use people you know or imagine to aid your character construction. Marlon Brando is said to have studied and adopted the characteristics of a gorilla for his portrayal

of Stanley Kowalski in *A Streetcar Named Desire* (Kazan, 1951), and a bulldog for *The Godfather* (Coppola, 1972).

The Method is useful as a starting point for the truth and to open your availability to possible emotions elicited by your interpretation of the script. It can act as an external trigger to help take you into an emotional arena, like a doorway, where you can then connect to the circumstances of the script. Once the camera rolls, however, you must stay with the events of the scene itself. After all, in the moment, you don't remember a feeling you once had, you experience it.

Having assembled an emotional palette from which your character's inner life can choose, you can use your past experiences as the character not the inner actor. Thinking of your dog Fluffy when you were six will be counterproductive and take you out of the scene. Of course, the ideal is to look at someone, fall in love with them within the cocoon of the script every time. That's the ideal and that's what you should work towards. However, if you are uninspired by take sixty-two it may be helpful to think about Fluffy. And if that doesn't work then you may have to fake it!

Many actors are dubious about the techniques used in method acting and are concerned about their safety and the possible tendency towards self-indulgent performances. My challenge to you is to try it and discover the uses, or otherwise, for yourself. At the same time, recognizing that your fellow performers may have a different approach.

Another footnote: there is a difference between the character lying and you lying. Feel free to make your characters the biggest liars that ever walked the planet and explore ways and means in which they attempt to cover up their lies. Let them never search for or find the truth and suffer the consequences.

TRUTH EXERCISE

Learn the lines for the following monologue and, without any further preparation, film yourself speaking them. For the purposes of this exercise Lizzie can be male or female.

INT. KITCHEN. DAY

We cut to all the staff of the house lined up in the big kitchen, the cooks, the maids, the flunkies. LIZZIE is facing them all, in his/her customary dark clothes. He/she is holding a clipboard and ticking off items as he/she covers them. We join him/her in mid-sentence as he/she addresses the staff.

LIZZIE ... Now you all know where you are going to be, you've got your positions – so keep to them. Don't wander off ... Concentrate all the time. (*She coughs.*) Excuse me, I have got a touch of flu ... (*She looks up, determined.*) But I am fine ... (*Sharp smile.*) Just don't come too close ... ! Now, as you know, coming to this party is everybody from Cabinet ministers to small children – I'm sure we will be able to tell the difference – (*She smiles.*) But just in case, there is a full list I'm putting up here, of everybody that is coming ... (*She stares at the staff.*) It makes interesting reading ...

- Now, work on the details, specifics and truth: the place, who you are talking to, the drawing up of the guest list and so forth. Truthfully feel the symptoms of the flu. Then film again.

- Compare the two, observe the differences and repeat as necessary.

- Go to https://vimeo.com/251794286 for an example.

20
THE SENSES AND SENSE MEMORY

The senses are powerful and give us context and place. Use yours to trigger emotional and physical memories to help you commit fully to the scene.

We use our senses to harvest information from and about the world around us. We rely on them to connect with each other and the wider world. They establish our place, and impact upon who we are at any particular moment. Whether you are watching a beautiful sunset, listening to birds chirping, feeling the sun against your skin, tasting the warmth of a brandy by a log fire or smelling the scent of Jasmine as you land at a foreign airport, your senses guide your mood and reawaken memories and experiences. In his poem 'The Rank Stench of Those Bodies Haunts Me Still', for instance, Siegfried Sassoon uses the senses to take us to the trenches of the First World War, our emotions being triggered by his sense memories. He talks of the stench of bodies, the smell of battle, the brown lines of tents with the snoring of men, and through his evocative language we smell, see, touch, hear and taste the horror of war as if we were there.

As an actor, you use your senses to establish yourself and the viewer in a scene. If you are freezing cold it will impact upon your state and ours. If you smell the stench of battle it will show in your physiology and emotional being and we will be affected by you being affected. A clear example of this is through the Chorus in Shakespeare's *Henry V* who has the job of painting the picture and describing the action for the audience. He talks about working on the imagination through the senses and his description transforms a bare stage into the sights and sounds of a living night before a battle, and he entices us to see the majestic English ships cutting a furrow to war in France. He uses your senses to persuade you that you are truly living in the imaginary circumstances of the script and participating in the action.

Different people may have one sense stronger than another. Radar operators and daytime sentries on patrol require an acute sense of sight, whereas a sentry on night duty may have a stronger sense of hearing. One sense can also trigger the onset of others. If you see a roast chicken, your brain may add the senses of smell and taste from the filing cabinet in your mind to the visual image. It is useful for you to consider which of yours is the most acute and develop the weaker ones. The exercises below will be of assistance.

Stanislavski introduced the concept of sense memory to the acting world. From his initial teachings, Meisner, Strasberg, Stella Adler et al. developed techniques to use our senses to establish place and mood and to recall emotions. Your senses invoke memories and evoke feelings and you can train them to do so. The smell of Elnett hairspray reminds me of my mother and the smell of Rive Gauche perfume of my first girlfriend. The sound of 'Yesterday' by the Beatles reminds me of my childhood and 'Happy' by Pharrell of my wife and kids. The sharp smell of a gentleman's public convenience has an immediate and altogether different reaction but, nevertheless, a real one.

How does the process work? Non-scientifically put, you see, hear, taste, smell and touch things and the stimuli are converted into electrical signals which carry to your brain. Your brain then pieces the information together – through the filter of your experience, knowledge and instinct – and produces a whole picture; potentially resulting in an impulse or reaction.

You may not be able to concentrate on all five (six if you include intuition) at the same time, but your senses are all always informing you of where and how you are, helping you stay in the middle of life and not merely in a scene in a film.

The Russian behavioural scientist Ivan Pavlov rang a bell every time he fed his dog so that the dog would salivate when he heard it even when there was no food around. In the same way, you can manipulate your senses to help your acting. Once again, preparation is the key. Creating the place – whether a room, restaurant or field – will help you forget that the crew is watching or that you are in a studio with a casting director, and will immediately take you into a scene. Focusing on the senses helps filter out the background noise and shines a spotlight onto the imaginary circumstances and what is relevant. I was invited to audition for a feature film where the action in the scene took place around a dinner table. I decided I had regularly eaten there so, to prepare, I worked on my Aunt Rene's home where I used to go for dinner as a child. I saw the salt and pepper cellars, the soup terrine, paintings and so forth. By using my sense memory, I prepared for the taste of chicken soup to enter my mouth and the smell to enter my nostrils. At the audition, after a little chit chat, the casting director suggested we start the scene. I immediately smelt the soup and connected to the salt cellar on Aunt Rene's table. As a result, by focusing on specific narrowly defined senses, I was immediately in the scene and not in a room in West London.

A sense of place

By focusing on the place where the action occurs you will bring it immediately into the focus of your brain. If you tell yourself that you are in a doctor's surgery and have worked on visualizing and creating the walls, ceiling and floor, you can crash zoom into this world and believe that you are there – a by-product being that you will not feel as if you are in a studio with a film crew around you.

A place is not neutral. It has an impact on what you do and how you feel. If you are in a court room or an immigration holding cell at an airport, you will feel differently than if you were lying on a sunny beach, in your mother's bedroom, your first partner's bedroom, the place you first made love, the place you broke up with your first true love, a sports stadium packed with your fellow supporters or in the opposition supporters' end.

Your relationship with a place is also important and a king in his throne room feels and behaves very differently to how a servant does. Thus, by mentally manipulating space you can affect your status level and connection with others in the room. If you want to feel strong and powerful when going into an audition, be the king entering his throne room to a trumpet fanfare.

You may also mentally bring someone else into your place, or position them on the outside, to strongly influence your state of being. Standing next to, but outside, Hannibal Lecter's cage will generate different physical, mental and spiritual impulses than if you were on the inside with him. Or the same with the film *Panic Room* where Jodie Foster was hiding in a room with the baddies on the outside trying to get in.

Ensure that you rehearse within and acquaint yourself with the space until it becomes as familiar as if it were really your own. If it is to be your kitchen, practise making tea, opening the drawers, taking spoons out, sitting and rising from the chairs and so on.Your brain needs to have the familiarity, freedom, muscle memory and habitual movement so it can concentrate on something else, i.e. the circumstances of the script. Knowing your constraints then freely working within them, you will have spatial awareness and be free to move how your impulses take you in the moment.

Specify certain parts of the space. A corner may remind you of where you had to stand for hours on end when you were a kid and may generate an emotional response from a deep-seated part of you. A tree may remind you of your first kiss. Be really specific and then rest the memories in your subconscious to be connected with the script and utilized by your inner character if and when necessary.

In situation comedies, the place is essential to the action and is often a character in its own right. The bar in *Cheers* is more important than any of the characters and their relationships are dictated by it; who sits where, the use of the phone, the entrances and exits. New ones come and go and are interchangeable, but the place remains the same.

SENSE MEMORY EXERCISES

The breakfast drink

The breakfast drink is the first in a series of exercises and is extremely useful for focus and concentration. There will also be times in auditions and on the set when you need to imagine that you are holding an object which is either not there or is not the real object but a prop. As you must not fake it or be doing an exercise in the middle of a scene, with this practice you can convince your brain that you are holding it, as *if* it were there. You will stay in the scene rather than your brain thinking *what the hell are they playing at, that's not a wine goblet it's a green plastic cup!*

When you see an actor carrying a supposedly full suitcase, which you can clearly see is empty, it takes you right out of the action. Or when a supposedly full coffee cup is handed over in such a way that if it were indeed full the recipient would be scalded by the hot liquid!

Every morning for two weeks, make a hot drink, find a comfortable spot and sensorially explore and examine the cup. Very slowly, for five minutes each, use one sense at a time and study it in detail. Study it; hear it – tap the cup or listen to the liquid gently moving around – feel it by slowly moving your fingertips, practically one cell at a time; smell it by allowing the flavours of the cup and liquid to enter your nostrils; and lick the cup and allow the liquid inside to cover your taste buds. Having explored each sense, put the cup aside and notice the existence of the sense. Take your time and let the senses come to you, don't chase them. After doing this for 25 minutes, set the cup aside and hold it as if it was still there. It may be tricky at first but keep with it as the more you do it the easier it becomes. Feel the weight of the *as if* cup in your hand, see and hear it, and allow the smells and tastes to come to you.

Go to https://vimeo.com/251794362 for a demonstration on how to do the breakfast drink.

Mirror exercise

Slowly study yourself in a mirror for a good few minutes. Then step to the side and continue seeing and studying yourself *as if* the mirror were still there.

Keep practising until it becomes easier, then, if you wear make-up slowly apply it, or if you shave, slowly do that. Take your time. Don't push, pantomime or fake it but really see yourself as if you are putting on the makeup or shaving.

This is a useful exercise on many levels, not least for when you have to look down the lens of the camera as if you are looking in the mirror or at a TV.

Go to https://vimeo.com/251795537 for a demonstration of how to do the mirror exercise.

Three pieces of material

Find three distinct and contrasting types of material – like silk, denim or wire wool – and, as with the above exercises, slowly and fully explore them one sense at a time; see, feel, smell, taste and hear them. Put them aside and sensorially allow them to be available to you.

This is a useful exercise when you are wearing costumes which are not made of the materials they are supposed to represent, e.g. heavy suits of armour which are actually made of plastic or light fabric.

Or, if you need to feel sexy in a scene imagine you are wearing silk close to your skin. Try it and see how well it works for you.

Sharp smell/taste

Taking your time again, see, touch, smell and taste a lemon. Put it aside and allow the lemon senses to come back to you. Repeat with a different contrasting item, such as bleach or ammonia – not tasting it, of course! These exercises have many practical and frequent uses – for example, when playing detectives, CSI investigators or suchlike roles and you are tasting and smelling evidence which are, in reality, innocuous props but are meant to elicit powerful sensorial reactions.

Overall sensations

Sun – Stand, sit or lie in the warm sun and bask in it – this may be tricky if you live in the UK! Feel it against your skin, smell and taste it. Step out of the sun, close your eyes and allow the sensations to return to. Notice how your mood changes when you feel the *as if* sun against your skin.

Do the exercise even if you have no sun where you are. You may be surprised how much your senses and muscles remember the experience from previous occasions.

This is especially useful at auditions, on a set or in a studio when the weather or climate is different than in the script. Also when standing on a crowded train and you want to be anywhere else!

Bath – Lie in a warm bath. Feel the water against your skin, hear the movement of the water and so forth. After about 15 minutes, get out, dry yourself off, find a place to lie down and sensorially recreate the sensation of being in the bath.

The practical uses of this exercise can be the same as with the sun above.

– Lie in a cold bath and notice the different sensations.

Fine misty rain – Following the same process as above, stand in the rain or spray your face with a household water spray device.

Fantasy overall sensation – Imagine, sensorially, that you are in the bath and it begins to fill with blood, then with jelly, custard or suchlike. Then with cockroaches and other creepy crawlies – this can be a useful practical exercise if you are playing a heroin addict going through withdrawal or someone who is massively uncomfortable in their skin.

Go to https://vimeo.com/251795623 for a demonstration of the overall sensations of sun and rain.

AUDIO EXERCISES

- Practise listening to music on headphones then remove them and listen as if the music is still there.

- Listen to animal sounds and do the same.
- Listen to music of different genres allowing yourself to be affected by it. Reflect on how you may use this in your work – for example, what happens to your physicality and mood with heavy rock music, punk or soul.

PLACE EXERCISE

Use a real place, such as your living room or bedroom, and ensure that you have peace, quiet and time to practise. Explore the room using all your senses, one by one, taking plenty of time over each. Slowly, as if cell by cell, feel the walls, the pictures on the walls, everything. Slowly introduce your other senses to fully immerse yourself in the space, allowing them to be *learnt* by your body.

Then move away from the place and allow the senses to come back to you. Don't push or go towards them but let them come to you. Change the place and use indoor and outdoor locations.

Practise for a week as, once again, the more you do it the easier it becomes. Then, without the need for it to make sense, recite a monologue or talk about nothing in particular. You will invariably be using dialogue in scenes, so it is good practice to speak out when the exercises become easier.

Once it comes more easily to you, as with the fantasy overall sensation exercise above, allow your imagination to change real places into fantasy ones. Maybe the walls turn into the silk of a desert tent with spices in the air; or they drip with blood; or begin to move or close in on you.

Explore your emotions, feelings and moods when experiencing these stimuli and note it down in your book for future use.

Go to https://vimeo.com/251813208 for a demonstration of a place exercise using memory and imagination.

Now do the same for inside Paul's mansion in *Friends and Crocodiles* in the scene below. See, feel, hear, smell and taste the place, taking in the atmosphere. Once you feel you are actually there, hear Paul's line in your head.

INT. PASSAGE IN THE BIG HOUSE. THE SAME DAY

PAUL opens a door in the passage. It reveals quite a large office, full of musty nineteenth-century furniture, box files going up to the ceiling and old metal filing cabinets.
Paul Will this do?

Now, experience the following in the same room from a little later in the script:

INT. LIZZIE'S ROOM. LATE AFTERNOON

LIZZIE working in her office; everything is tidy now, and there is order in the room … There is a sense that a little time has passed, maybe 3 weeks. From her window she has a good view over the garden, at this particular moment just BUTTERWORTH is meandering about on the lawn. A bell suddenly starts ringing, an old hand yanked bell. It is coming from somewhere in the room, but LIZZIE can't see where. She pulls the curtain back, it's not there. She moves towards the rusty old filing cabinet, the bell gets louder. She yanks and pulls the cabinet back, to reveal a series of old servants' bells covered in dust and cobwebs: one of the bells is clanging, rasping out. As she stares at it, the one next to it begins to ring too.

Play around with this. Add and change overall sensations; add a sharp taste; bring one sense in and then another … and enjoy doing it!

21
THINKING AND THE INNER MONOLOGUE

Strong and vivid thinking gives power to your performances and makes them more real and interesting.

It is important to point out that everyone thinks in their own unique way. Some see their thoughts in images as a movie, colours or mood board, while others may read them like lines. Thoughts fight for position, roll over on top of and cut across and through each other. They slow down and speed up, are short as well as long, are good and bad, boring, funny or sad. They ebb and flow, wax and wane and stumble and ramble. There is an attempt at discipline and a desire for freedom, a longing for calmness and a heat of passion. Essentially, there are a myriad of them and they are as uncontrollable as wild stallions yet manageable and capable of order.

An image comes from an object or colour outside your head and goes into your brain through the eyes. The brain then searches its memory banks to work out what the object is and your relationship to it. If you see a tiger running towards you, your brain will have a get-the-hell-out-of-here flight instruction which it sends to the rest of your body, whereas if there is an attractive association with the image it may recommend you move closer.

If someone asks you a question it follows a similar pattern, this time channelling the information to your brain through your ears rather than your eyes. Your brain then explores your storage area and data banks, identifies possibilities and comes up with an opinion. There are a huge amount of resultant options and available choices ranging from the ridiculous to the eminently sensible and doable. Your experience and instinct will hopefully choose the right one for you and it all happens in an instant. If you slow the film down, you will identify much of this process as *thinking*.

Your senses play a huge part and each one has its own storage section and suggested responses. The sound of a gunshot will force you onto the ground even though you may not see the shooter, the sound of your lover gently whispering in the dark may arouse you differently, as the heat from a fire will tell you not to get too close to it.

Working on your thinking is a smart move and the more informed you can make it by packing your filing system with research, preparation and character experiences, the better. Having strong character opinions and choices helps enable great acting and the more choices of thought and actions you can make, the more colourful and spontaneous your performances will be.

Thinking and the eyes

There are many acting classes where you are told to just look your scene partner deeply in the eye and talk. However, people don't do that in real life. On a purely practical level, if you are walking along the road staring in your friend's eyes as you talk, you will undoubtedly bump into something or get run over.

Staring is not a welcomed trait in many societies either and is mostly done to elicit a specific effect, such as intimidation or deep longing.

Also, people avoid looking at each other for very good reasons. You may not want to look the other person in the eye because you are lying and are concerned they may see through your lies. Or you think they are gorgeous but are too shy to let them know.

Your eyes are always in focus on something whether a memory or someone or something tangible in front of you. There are occasions when you look into your mind to search for an answer and your eyes leave the subject and move up or down. They change their focus and even dull a little. You go into that large universe of your brain with your whole attention placed upon what you are thinking and talking about rather than anything superfluous like the camera. You became immersed in it and the creative side of your brain fills the space.

Think of any of your favourite movies or TV programs and there will undoubtedly be scenes where the story is driven forward by the character's thinking. The director and editor will often hold focus on the listener more than the speaker. We are left to figure out their opinion on the event as they silently contemplate what has, or is going to happen. Two of my favourite examples are Anthony Hopkins in *The Human Stain* (Benton, 2003) and Michael Kitchen in the TV series *Foyle's War* (Horowitz, 2002–15), where their thinking is so clear and strong that they seem to be constantly on the verge of speaking their thoughts out loud. But don't because it's not in the script.

A kaleidoscope of thought

Acting is not simply setting objectives and actions for a scene, single-mindedly focusing on the other person and honing your whole attention on the words being spoken to you. It is not about purely asking *what is your objective*? Indeed, focusing on a single objective can run you into an acting cul-de-sac.

Objectives create movement and are essential within life and within a scene. They seek for and instigate change in you, your partners, the scenario and the viewer, shifting behaviour, beliefs and relationships. But they are almost never a conscious single thought and fixating on them may have the opposite effect than you intend. Human beings do not doggedly focus in the moment on why they are doing something or having a conversation with someone, nor do they constantly consider what they want from it. As you are reading this you are not consciously thinking of your objective in reading it. You knew what it was when you bought, borrowed, downloaded or stole the book but have probably not thought about it much since. While I am writing, I am not thinking of my objective. When I decided to write a book, I set my objective as passing on my experiences and thoughts to interested people who could be positively influenced by them. However, it would be weird if I was sitting here all the time focusing on that. The truth is that I never think about it, it is just there. My objective was set up strongly enough at the beginning so as to motivate the thoughts which I am putting down on paper.

Also, life is random and messy, and we think multiple thoughts concurrently in the same moment; like broadband with a host of information simultaneously passing through the pipe. Life is not a binary straight line. If you were hooked up to a brain scanner we would see a huge amount of activity firing off. It's what I like to call a *kaleidoscope of thought*. While you have been reading this chapter, you have been thinking of other things as well as what is on the page in front of you. You may have remembered to do a household chore, call a friend or relate the text to a previous conversation or book you have read. But your objective is still the same.

It is totally acceptable to think about other things while you are in the scene. If it is your inner character thinking multiple thoughts all the better. But if your inner actor pops in with an unrelated brain fart such as *I wonder what my call time will be tomorrow*, recognize that this happens, stay loose and know you will return. Without this freedom, you will tense up and fall down the rabbit hole. As with most things in life, what is important is the recovery and developing ways of snapping yourself back to your inner character's thoughts and experiences (see chapter on *focus and concentration*). If the frame has been set for your close-up and you are thinking clearly and strongly enough then all will be well. The viewer does not and cannot read exactly what you are thinking. They will make their own assumptions based on their perception of the information provided in the script to date and their take on the universe at that moment in time.

There is a firework display going off in your head with multiple thoughts randomly popping up. In a conversation with a potential mate you may have a lot of thoughts all flashing at the same time. You may question whether they are a potential life partner, whether you want to have sex with them and what it would be like if you did; you might remember your parents' tough relationship, what it was like on your first ever date, whether you have enough money to start a relationship, kids and so forth.

Working on objectives must be through the inner actor in preparation and left alone by the inner character. A fully functioning inner character will be working just like in real life and you must help yours function smoothly through your preparation. Work in rehearsal on as many potential thoughts as possible and place them in your subconscious to be used, or not, when the time comes.

In an instant, multiple similar and opposing objectives create a tension of contrasting energies and resistance within your mind, like placing the positive end of a battery next to a negative one. You love and hate at the same time and feel anxious and exhilarated. Thoughts come and go and moods change in an instant. One thought creates another which may be unusual, unpredictable or random. One new image may change your relationship to what came before. Thinking of an apple may remind you of Snow White or Isaac Newton, either of which will then set off different reactional thought processes.

We explored this in the chapter on *adjusting vocal levels*, but speed of thought is not necessarily connected to speed of delivery and you must be wary of talking too quickly when thinking fast.

The freedom gained by knowing that your thinking is complex and personal may loosen up your preparation and relieve the pressure. You don't always need to know exactly what and why you are thinking, so you can discover and explore places unforeseen at the start. You don't do it in life so why force yourself into this box when performing?

There are, of course, technical considerations which must be considered and practised. I cover this a little in the chapter *size matters*, but there is a host of available material out there to help. For example, on an extreme close-up with your face filling most of the screen it is very distracting for the viewer if you look from eye to eye like we sometimes do in real life. It comes across as *too big*, so you need technique to lessen our discomfort; such as looking at only one of your scene partner's eyes or at their forehead when talking to them. As an exercise, practise this and make it a habit.

Michael Caine's rather dated book and video on screen acting, *Acting in Film* (2000), has some useful tips (as well as some clunky ones). For example, use your eye furthest away from the camera on a close-up or medium shot to look at your scene partner's eye closest to the camera. This will open your face towards the camera and allow the viewer to see your thoughts more clearly.

A third entity

Life happens in at least three dimensions. As it moves forward in time and place it is heavily influenced by occurrences and activities from all sides, both within and outside the action. While you are talking to me about what you want for lunch you may also be thinking about an intense discussion you had earlier with your partner. You may be so concentrated on the event outside the scene that you only have a limited capacity left to concentrate on whether you want the meat or fish.

This is what I call a *third entity*: something which is not present in the scene but which has a major impact on it. The external existence of a mistress, illness or a shiny new car has an impact on what you are feeling and thinking in the moment and, therefore, has an impact on your actions and reactions with other characters.

The third entity is a useful tool when working on character thoughts so fill your stock of them as full as possible with the time you have available to work on it. While you are rehearsing a scene, focus as much as possible on a third/external component. Change the component and see how the scene is affected. Then put them all aside and trust they are in the mix somewhere.

Inner monologue

An inner monologue is what it says on the tin; a story you tell or conversation you have which is silent and inside your head. It can stand by itself or as a reaction to what is being said by others. It could even be considered as an inner soliloquy. It impacts your reactions, your desires, everything. It can be a gentle internal whisper, a violent shouting rage or anything in-between. The louder the inner monologue the more visible it can be to the viewer, whereas the subtler it is the more the viewer must work to uncover what is going on. We may be on tenterhooks or surprised by the character's reactions. During the monologue in *The Godfather II* (Coppola, 1974) when Diane Keaton is telling Al Pacino that she has had an abortion and wants to leave him, the smouldering force of his thoughts and opinions precedes a violent reaction. The strength of his inner monologue builds and builds and drives the scene forward to its violent conclusion.

EXERCISE

Work on and record the following inner monologue in a medium close up. Prepare as if you are learning a script with dialogue but focus on thinking your thoughts alone in isolation. Fill your head full of Angela/Alan's opinions and film it. If you would like, you can also include the stage direction of sipping your latte; as long as you practise seamlessly incorporating it. Make very clear choices on the people, places and events involved and make them real to yourself.

Ask a friend to read in the announcements when they feel they are appropriate, or time and record them yourself to play back with the necessary gaps. Make the context and subject matter gender relevant – Michael becoming Michaela. The actual inner monologue starts from the *EVENT*, sitting in the station studying your laptop.

SET UP: Angela/Alan Harper is a working mother/father of an 11-year-old daughter, Jayne. S/he is going through a messy divorce from her/his husband/wife of fourteen years, Michael/a. Angela has been called to a meeting in Brussels by her biggest client, Global Health (a pharmaceuticals company), who are about to launch a new drug to combat the early onset of MS. In the *Financial Times* yesterday was a report that Global's German competitor, Vulcan, had completed clinical trials of a similar drug and three patients had come down with symptoms leading to their heads swelling up 'like the elephant man'.

Michael/a moved out from the family home in Barnsbury and has moved into a bachelor/ette flat in Notting Hill. Angela's mother is a frequent babysitter and lives in Edgware but her recent health is causing concern and she is becoming less mobile.

Angela has an excellent relationship with Global but this is a vital time for their business and everyone is very nervous. If the product is given clearance by the European Medical Agency it will mean $1 billion in sales and a rosy future. If it does not then job losses and closures will ensue.

Angela's main contact at Global, Juliette, called yesterday at 5.00 pm for her to come over to Brussels for a hastily arranged review meeting and Angela arranged for her mum to pick Jayne up from the school bus today and babysit and send her off to school in the morning.

PRE-EVENT: Wednesday morning. Angela woke at 6.00 am, got Jayne ready for school, had a full day's work at the office preparing for the meeting, left for St Pancras train station for the Eurostar to Brussels, and cleared immigration at 3.45 for a 4.25 train. She immediately becomes immersed in the legal documents on the clinical trials on her laptop.

EVENT: I spot a couple of typos which I correct and save. These documents have taken nine months to prepare; 1,800 pages and I am pretty sure that they are about right. I spot another simple mistake and save it thinking that I will send the updated version to Juliette before I get into the tunnel.

TRAIN ANNOUNCEMENT

'The 4.25 to Brussels is now boarding from gate 2.'

I know there is no rush, spot another correction and save it. Satisfied, I sip my latte. It's a good job I noticed that last correction as it could have resulted in a two-week delay.

I like Brussels. I remember the last time I went with Jayne and took her to the Magritte Museum. Jayne loved all those funny men with the bowler hats and the apples. I liked the cracked sky paintings myself. They really appealed to me because of my divorce. Maybe Jayne will be an artist when she is older? She really likes painting and is actually pretty good at it. Maybe she will go into advertising? Or be unemployed? Artists can go either way! We should go to Barcelona next. We could fly. She's never been on a plane. She'd love it … oh, no … I forgot!! Jayne is going on a school trip today and is being dropped back at school after the school bus has left! I forgot to tell my daughter that I wasn't going to be there to pick her up! I didn't tell Michael I was going away. My mum is going to meet her from the school bus at the end of the road and babysit but she won't know what to do if Jayne is not on the bus. (I take out my phone and call my mum's number). It rings and rings. No reply! Why doesn't she get an answer machine? (I hang up and call my mum's mobile). This goes to a message saying the 'phone is switched off, please call back later'. Why can't she switch her phone on? I tell her and tell her, but she never listens!

TRAIN ANNOUNCEMENT

'Will the last remaining passengers for the 4.25 to Brussels please make their way immediately to gate 2.'

Michael. I can't call him. The last time I spoke to him I told him he was a rubbish father and he should drop dead! I can't ask him for a favour. He'd never let me live it down. His lawyer would use it to get back at me. But he'd ask me. Oh yes, he'd ask me. He would have no qualms at all about that. Selfish … What to do? I can't cancel Brussels. Brussels! My god, this could be my job! And lots of other people's jobs too! I have to call Michael. Take a deep breath. (I dial his number). And get his answer machine. I can't leave a message! (I hang up).

TRAIN ANNOUNCEMENT

'The gate for the 4.25 to Brussels is now closing. Any further passengers must make their way immediately to gate 2.'

What should I do? I can still get to Jayne's school if I leave now. But what about my meeting? Juliette will be mad. It's a huge amount of business! (pick up phone again and start to dial a number) ... cut.

- When reviewing the footage, you may think that your face is moving a lot or that you are doing too much. If you are really in it then all is justified, because, as a human, you move your eyebrows, rub your face, tap your fingers, twirl pens around in your hand and remove and replace your glasses. In fact, try not doing it and see how hard it is. Watch people on the train or bus and see how much they move.

- Notice the moments you thought you were out when you were recording but it looked like you were in on the playback.

- Consider how much you noticed the camera or otherwise.

Go to https://vimeo.com/251797118 for a demonstration with the same script.

EXERCISE – STRONG THOUGHT

Pick something you could have a strong opinion about but which your scene partner – or a mark at the side of the camera – has the opposing view. It could be that you are brother and sister at the reading of your father's will, or that your partner has been unfaithful. Fill your head full of your character's thoughts and silently think the argument and the stream of consciousness from your side of the conversation. Record yourself for about a minute going from 1 to 10 in terms of loudness of the thoughts in your head. At 10, really scream in your head; at 1, really whisper. Then review the footage.

Go to https://vimeo.com/251797270 for a demonstration.

EXERCISE

Film and review yourself searching inside your head for the details of a story. It can be the last time you went shopping if you like. Think of all the minutiae: which aisle you walked down, which products you picked up and so forth.

EXERCISE

- Film yourself doing *general acting* thinking pretending that you hate or love someone.
- Now, film yourself truthfully thinking about someone real whom you have a strong opinion about.
- Compare the two.

22

IMPROVISE AND PERSONALIZE

Support the truth in a scene using improvisation and personalization.
Establish reality, context and specificity.

Improvisation is the creation and execution of actions and words in the moment without a prior set plan. The circumstances are often given but the words and their use are your own. Improvisation can be divided into two categories: *external* and *internal*.

External improvisation is what you do with other actors to deepen your understanding of character, relationships and circumstances. Advanced by the Commedia dell'Arte in sixteenth-century Italy, it has become a particularly useful tool in rehearsal for both screen and theatre work. The more context created around a script and the more you develop shared experiences and memories with your fellow cast members to inform and enrich your performances, the more truthful, complete and colourful your performance will be.

Improvisation is a useful way of creating context and breadth but, due to lack of time, resources and availability of fellow cast members, it is not always possible to improvise around enough of the script. Through *internal* improvisation you can consciously create memories and events as if they have really occurred and reinforce them using sense memory and fantasy. By employing your imagination, you can conduct this internal improvisation on your own, inventing and living the circumstances in your mind as if they were real. Close your eyes, see it like a movie being played out in your head, watch the action unfold and place yourself within it. Think of it like virtual reality which allows your user interaction within an artificially replicated environment. Create a sensory experience which includes sight, sound, touch, taste and smell but, rather than using a headset, omni-directional treadmill or special gloves, you use your cognitive faculties. Reality changes as the environment does and you can move around wherever your imagination takes you. Repeat the improvisation enough times for you to strengthen your experiences into belief, after which they can be stored and made use of at will.

The significance of this internal improvisation manifests itself once the scene begins. If it starts with you ringing the doorbell of your ex-partner who you have not seen since you were put in prison for breaking a restraining order, you will need to be in the appropriate mental and physical state before you press it; possibly for multiple takes. It will help to have the experiences of your life with your partner in the back of your mind; specific instances of falling in and out of love with them, and the fighting and hate which has led you to this moment. The pressing of the doorbell becomes a trigger and entrance into a meaningful and unknown future event rather than a meaningless and perfunctory action.

The beginning of a scene in a play or on-screen is often regarded as difficult to seamlessly move into and from. Going from a neutral place to the correct emotional, physical or vocal pitch of a scene can instigate a gearing up to where you think you should be. This can require a lot of work in the brief time between *roll camera* and *action* and may leave a fertile ground for your saboteur to feed on any tension and cause you to push and overact. Seamlessly entering this next phase of your life (the scene) can be eased by specific preparation on the physical and emotional journey leading up to the moment of pressing the bell and a smooth transition into it. At the beginning of the scene you don't start performing. Your inner character continues feeling what they were already feeling. Your character is thinking about what is happening to you/them rather than, *should I start now?*

Whether you are about to shoot or *cut* has been called, you are not in a scene but in the middle of life. If you are truly *in it*, the words *action* and *cut* will merely be extraneous sounds and won't affect how you are feeling or what you are doing. Your inner actor registers the words but is not impacted by them. At the end of a traumatic scene you should feel dreadful. At the end of a love scene you may be feeling horny. Obviously, this is where you need to consciously switch off so you don't get yourself in trouble.

Improvise the journey and circumstances in your mind. See yourself sitting in your prison cell night after night, day after day obsessing over the first time you will meet your ex again. Are they having an affair? Have they forgotten you? Do they hate you? Are her friends advising her to dump you forever? Will love be enough to conquer all? The more specific and clear examples you put in your mind, the more solid the foundation of your presence will be.

Personalization of the world of the script will cement this further. By imagining the person you are meeting as someone you know in your real life, your emotional response will be real and even stronger; especially if your experience with them is appropriate – maybe they broke off your relationship and never explained why? Think of the big loves in your life and allow yourself to lose them again. Go back to the times you met and when you dated. Then argue with them in your mind about important and unimportant matters. Stay close to the circumstances of the script, take your time and create the whole world. Once it has bedded in and you believe it, take the journey in your mind from the prison to the front door and allow yourself to think the character's thoughts along the way. If you are on a bus, see the other passengers. Maybe you feel as if they are all watching you? Or looking straight through you? If you drove then see, hear, smell and feel the car. Pick a car which you already know rather than starting from scratch and reinventing the wheel. If it has an emotional content all the better; maybe one you bought with your ex-partner or one which constantly broke down.

The type of car may also affect your state of mind or physicality when you arrive. If you imagine yourself in a Rolls-Royce, you will be in a different frame of mind than if you are in a battered-up heap of junk. Add even more specificity by internally improvising and seeing the route taken. If the scene starts with you arriving in Brooklyn by taxi having driven from Manhattan, from the comfort of your own home you can input the start location and destination on sites such as Google Earth and view the journey from one place to the next. Notice what you see around you; how many traffic lights you stop at, any vacant burnt-out buildings, luxury apartments, prisons, bars etc. Have a conversation with the taxi driver and as you're driving along think about the last time you were there and the last time you saw the person you are visiting.

Once you have improvised a few times in your mind you can cut corners. First time out you may need to see the whole journey but in subsequent improvisations you may shorten the movie and just see the milestones through images, sounds or smells along the way.

In the restaurant scene from *Kramer vs Kramer* which I referred to earlier, Ted's mental and physical journey between receiving Joanna's phone call request to meet up and arriving at the restaurant is essential for his entry into the scene and where he went with it. Through his mental preparation, Hoffman was able to be spontaneous and own the impulses which Ted could have had in this situation. When he smashes the glass against the wall at the end of the scene it was totally real, unforced and not in the script.

Likewise, in the same scene, Meryl Streep talks about seeing a therapist in LA and sitting in a coffee shop opposite the school watching her son Billy playing. She really needs to believe that these events took place otherwise her brain would be going *what is she talking about, that never happened*, and she would have dropped out. Improvising the action in her head to make it real for herself will also make it real for Ted and us.

If you are playing Joanna you must make the therapy sessions real. Imagine in detail the therapist's building, waiting room, receptionist and office and improvise the conversations in your mind. Talk through your issues with the therapist and see your progress. Not only will this be effective for the context of the scene but it will also give you more information on Joanna, as you have to think in detail about her inner life and hidden secrets. This will take time but it is an integral part of her journey and, therefore, the scene itself.

As for the coffee shop, think of a real one which you are familiar with and imagine sitting there looking out through a real window to a real school, which you may also be familiar with.

Clearly Billy, the son, is an integral part of the scene even though he is not in it. Both characters have a deep experience of their relationship with him, so you must too. See and experience the moment you found out you were pregnant, the birth, the various birthdays, the ups and downs and your separation from your life partner. If you have a child of your own use them in your mind's improvisation. If you don't, think of a young relative, a next-door neighbour, a friend's child or somebody from your past who means something to you. Then ramp up your feelings for them. See them coming out of school, notice the clothes they wear, do you remember buying them and if so from where. Or are they new?

You can convince your brain of anything you want and sometimes you must. You must really believe that you are on the bridge of the Starship *Enterprise* hurtling through space being chased by Klingons, and not on a set in the back of beyond with a green screen and a plastic phaser in your hand.

A lot of work goes into preparation and making scenarios real for yourself but you will already have people, places and things stored in your subconscious which will give you strong enough opinions on the subject matter. Use childhood places, people you love and detest, occasions when you were joyous or miserable, the times you tried to give up smoking, your first sexual encounter and so on and so forth. Write them all down in your notebook for future use.

It will help to have strong opinions on everything. If you hate your partner, *really* hate them, if you are jealous, be *really* jealous, if you miss them, *really* miss them to the point of heartache.

If you are trying to ignore their constant digs, repeat a mantra over and over in your head – *I will not let him win, I will not let him win*. As the mantra is the character's, this will keep your inner character to the fore.

You also need to understand what you are talking about. This may sound obvious but it's surprising how often it is skated over. If you are in a scene which talks about double entry bookkeeping, then you need to know something about double entry bookkeeping. You don't need to have an accountancy degree but you need to have a good sense of what it is. If you are discussing the principles of a combustion engine then your brain needs to know that you know what you're talking about. If you are playing Mozart it's pretty obvious that you need to know something about composing music.

A scene needs movement and change, like a living organism which grows by the moment from one thing into another. There is a beginning, middle and end through which the character's emotional journey travels. Don't miss the necessary stages, give yourself somewhere to go and don't play the end of the scene at the beginning. If Joanna and Ted begin the scene at the same pitch they end it then no one would watch. We would not sympathize with either character nor stand listening to them shouting at each other. Also, don't throw the kitchen sink at your performance and resist the desire to show everyone how much work you've done by displaying your emotions all at once.

A lot of work goes into making acting look easy, real and believable. There is so much to think about and do within a short period of time that it may feel a little overwhelming. However, as with the mountain climbing analogy in Part One, you do not have to, nor should you, do it all immediately or simultaneously. Work on one thing at a time and trust that it is all being logged in your filing cabinet. Each improvised experience becomes layered one on top of the other, like the side of a cliff where you see the different layers of rock which have accumulated over many thousands of years. One layer squashes down on top of the other until it creates a whole and forms a solid structure.

Joanna and Ted have a lot of history prior to the destruction of their relationship. Improvise, personalize and layer on the moments they met, fell in love and conceived their child. Then drip feed specific arguments and specific problems. Improvise and layer on the separation, the moments of grief, relief, happiness, sadness and regret. Trust that it all goes in, one experience layered on top of the other. Rehearse the meeting only smiling and not letting the other person see how they are affecting you. Then add an obvious hatred for what they are saying to you. Then do the scene just thinking of the child and so on. Keep each layer and place one on top of the other.

When the director calls *action* your head will be so filled with character thoughts that your actor ones will not have the space to enter.

The common feature running through the above is specificity. Specificity is your best friend and will keep you focused in the moment and the scene. Many of the most iconic lines in cinema were improvised and for them to be accepted and admired so widely the actors must have created their characters so specifically that we would believe the lines fitted:

- *You're gonna need a bigger boat – Jaws* (Spielberg, 1975)

- *You talking to me? – Taxi Driver* (Scorsese, 1976)

- *Hey, I'm walking here – Midnight Cowboy* (Schlesinger, 1969)

- *Here's Johnny – The Shining* (Kubrick, 1980)

EXERCISE

Personalize everyone in and around the following scene from *Friends and Crocodiles*. Imagine that you are Lizzie or Paul standing in the shadows watching. Choose strong personal images and have an opinion on everyone and everything. Identify the contents of the hamper and vary your opinions on them.

EXT. THE PICNIC. AFTERNOON

A wide shot of a magnificent table by the lake, under the shade of a giant cedar tree. A gold and white tablecloth, silver cutlery, and a series of beautiful picnic hampers decorated with flowers.

LIZZIE *is standing in the shadows.*

A line of flunkies are waiting by the table. One of them rings a dinner gong which sends a rumbling noise all over the grounds.

We cut to the group coming towards us, moving down to the lake, with the house behind them. COYLE, BUTTERWORTH, SNEATH, THE ALBERT BROTHERS, REDFERN, GRAHAM *and all the other guests and hangers on.*

There is a new addition too. ANGELA *and* CHRISTINE *walking together, but* CHRISTINE *is pushing a strikingly beautiful young girl,* RACHEL, *in a wheelchair. The girl looks no more than fourteen.*

PAUL *is standing in the shadows watching them approach. There are some young children in the party too.*

Time cut. We see all the guests opening their hampers, like opening Christmas presents. The glow from the red lining of the hampers on their faces, their eyes shining when they see the rich contents, the lobster, the finely cured ham, the bottles of drink. Several of the guests can't stop themselves beaming with spontaneous delight.

EXERCISE

Improvise in your mind the events which have led up to this picnic. See yourself ordering everything, sending out the invitations, checking on the weather and so forth. Notice how your inner character feels more complete.

EXERCISE

Layer on different opinions in the scene. For example, Lizzie is feeling both embarrassed and super confident; she believes in the opulence of it then doesn't; try falling in love with the various people then despise them; be jealous and layer that on; think of the consequences if it starts to rain, someone gets drunk and misbehaves, the rest of the food doesn't arrive, and so forth.

23
MEET YOUR CHARACTER

A guided meditation where you will meet and further understand your character.

The deeper you go into the motivations, needs and wants of your characters, the more effectively you will be able to represent and portray them. The list of characteristics, history, traits and experiences in Appendix 5 gives a good start but we will go deeper here. In this chapter, you will get the opportunity to meet and question the characters you work on and discover a conscious way of embodying and connecting with them.

EXERCISE

On the accompanying audio file, found at https://vimeo.com/251801989, I will lead you on a guided meditation like the one in Part One where you met your captain; but this time you will meet your character. If you are not in a production or working on a specific character at present, choose the last one you worked on or, even better, work on a new one, like Paul or Lizzie from *Friends and Crocodiles.*

The text for the journey can be found in Appendix 6 but it may be more effective at first, to have me guide you.

Find a comfortable place to sit, listen to the audio file and take your time. When you have finished the exercise make notes on the answers you received. The questions I ask are limited so, once you have practised a few times, ask any further questions you wish.

Practise walking around as the character and interrelate with the world. Go to places where no one knows you and experience real interactions. Go into shops and ask directions or on public transport. Be careful if you are playing a psychopath of course.

24

MIND, BODY AND SOUL (THOUGHT, PHYSIOLOGY AND EMOTION)

Connecting your thoughts with your body and emotions. Controlling the strength of your performances.

For the purposes of this chapter, your mind is your thoughts, your body your physiology and your soul is representative of your emotions, essence and spirit.

There is a strong and malleable connection between these three elements which influences everything you feel, do and are. The nature of the flow of energy between them creates, establishes and enhances the life force of your characters – your character's life force being the combination of their experience, goals, needs and wishes, what gives them purpose and drive and makes them unique. It makes you you and them them; it lives as an independent within, and as part of the community of its universe; it touches and is touched by others; it has an impact and feels impacted; and is neither static or still but fluid, spontaneous and mostly unpredictable.

The human brain is very powerful and has a major impact on what happens with the body. Psychosomatic illness, placebos, gearing yourself up to jump out of a plane and mothers lifting cars from their crushed children are all identifiable examples. A thought is triggered in the mind and interpreted through the filter of your experience to provoke the reaction of an emotion. It is then sent onwards as an impulse, interpreted again and responded to by the body, which in turn sends it back up to the mind. And this carries on in a circular motion, like a vortex which picks up speed as it goes. This circular motion accumulates and builds emotion along the way so that you get angrier and angrier the more you think about something annoying or hornier and hornier when you ponder on something sexual.

If you act from the neck up (only intellectually, in your head) and don't involve your body and soul, you limit the prospect of feeling what the character is feeling and, more often than not, this will force you to fake and push. Your brain knows that you are performing to an audience and as it does not register a true physical or emotional signal it will act out the feeling. It says, *screw up your face because you're supposed to be in pain; laugh because something is supposed to be funny; make sobbing noises because it is sad.* This is the sort of acting that you see in amateur dramatics with untrained actors who have little or no technique or talent but lots of desire to entertain.

In some cultures, people are taught to not feel or express their emotions and to maintain a stiff upper lip. But as an actor this is the death of real and believable acting. The physiological flow connected to thought and emotion helps make your performance colourful and must be unblocked and unconstrained. If you do not allow yourself to feel an emotional response to the stimuli that are presented, your character will not be able to either. They will be unable to go with, or fight against and hide it, and consequently, you will restrict the chances of them serving the script.

So, you must feel. Keeping an accessible emotional pathway and an exercised body and mind are important components of your instrument. Give yourself permission to break emotional and physical logjams and prepare a free and open palette from which to paint; with multiple and varied thoughts, physical actions, reactions and feelings. Otherwise your performances run the risk of being thin and one dimensional.

Scripts usually have a strong emotional content and the strengths and levels involved are intrinsic to how the project will be presented to the viewer. It is possible to manipulate this holy trinity of mind, body and soul to facilitate the creation of different levels of intensity and strengths of reactions and feelings. Below are a few tools which can help you achieve this.

The pressure cooker

Earlier, I touched upon disciplining yourself to prevent unconnected movements and actions from dispersing your emotions, rather than retaining them and allowing the pressure which is building within your character to grow. In life, for good reasons, we mainly try to calm down and reduce this pressure. But in your craft as an actor you need to keep and even increase it. I equate it to doing the opposite of how a pressure cooker works.

Whereas a pressure cooker has a valve on the top which releases the steam (pressure) to prevent the pot from blowing up, you must keep yours in and let it build until it's ready to pop. And then keep it in some more.

Extraneous and unnecessary physical twitching or movement, and unconnected sighs and vocal ticks, produces the equivalent of a release of the steam and results in the leakage and loss of emotion from the stew of the mind, body, spirt cycle.

If you are involved in a scene where the other actor is pushing all your buttons but you must not show them your inner tension, the viewer will empathize with you more if they accompany you on your journey. However, if you don't feel the build-up of the emotion as you are leaving the good stuff on the floor or in the ether, they cannot.

Leonardo DiCaprio exploding as he is being discovered as a fraud near the end of *The Great Gatsby* (Luhrmann, 2013) is a clear example. He loses his temper and control and physically attacks his antagonist.

Unnecessary toe tapping under the table, unconnected glances off camera, pacing up and down and twitching of thumbs will dissipate your character's emotional energy leaving little at the end of the scene of any value or use. Premeditated and inappropriate-in-the-moment movement creates a break in the energy and a loosening of the taught string which runs from the start of the scene to the end.

If you find yourself moving unconnectedly mid-scene and recognize the need for control, find a reason for your inner character to control the movements, not your inner actor. Have your character keep still, like a poker player, not giving the other characters an inkling of what you are thinking and feeling. Of course, however hidden, if you feel it the camera will pick it up and the viewer will get a sense of it.

In the earlier restaurant scene from *Kramer vs Kramer*, the pressure builds so strongly on Ted that the only thing he can do at the end is explode. The same is true of the *Godfather II* scene where Michael explodes and hits his wife, Kay. He stays still, the emotion builds, his thoughts intensify, impacting his physiology, until the cooker explodes, and he hits her.

By turning your emotional dial up or down, the pressure cooker also allows you to control the level of your emotional response; like an adjustable furnace able to burn on full power driving your mental, physical and emotional machine forwards or backwards.

Emotion through physical manipulation

Very often you will be required to enter a scene at an intense emotional level. One way of reaching this heightened pitch is to focus on and identify physical and emotional feelings within your body and play with them.

When working on an emotional script, having completed your initial prep work, to reach an appropriately intense pitch identify where in your body you feel it. There may be a dull ache in your chest or solar plexus, a tension around the mid-rift or a stiff neck and shoulders. Once you have identified the sensation, consciously double its intensity, give it a few seconds then consciously double it again. Keep going until you reach bursting point then connect with the circumstances of the script. Connect with the love, hatred or sadness that the person opposite evokes in you and go with the scene. If the power and force is real you can hold back or not, depending upon what is required, and the viewer will be able to experience your inner struggle with you.

EXERCISE

When seeing Paul in the *Friends and Crocodiles* scene below, focus in on where you feel the physical sensation in your body. Is it in your chest, solar plexus or gut? Then concentrate and double the feeling to intensify your condition. Then double it again.

See https://vimeo.com/251802351 for demonstration.

EXERCISE – THE ROUNDABOUT

Another way of powerfully manipulating your emotional state whilst keeping within the realms of truth and reality, is centred around the idea of placing a collection of personal thoughts and experiences on a children's roundabout – the circular ones that are pushed or pulled and spun around at variable speeds:

- Imagine a children's roundabout which is divided, like a pie, into six sections.

- Place someone or something intensely personal on each of the sections which makes you sad, angry, frustrated or otherwise – it may be your partner, sibling, sick puppy or Adolf Hitler. If the scene is at the funeral of a loved one, put loved ones from your real life on some of the sections and the characters from the script on the rest.

- Work on the reasons for the intense emotion you feel, such as them being super annoying, dead or in a hospital bed.

- Then, with the items clear and specific, spin the roundabout slowly in your mind. As you feel it picking up speed and the emotional intensity increasing, you may begin to feel it in your body.

- Spin it faster …

- and faster …

- and faster, until you feel an appropriately intense strength of emotion; maybe as your pressure cooker is about to blow.

- Then connect fully to the circumstances in the script by giving your total attention to them. Superimpose your opinions of the characters and events and link them with how you feel in your mind, body and soul.

- Notice how you are affected. You will think, feel and act like a real person in a heightened emotional state and consequently have no space for the inner actor to upset the balance.

EXERCISE

The following scene from *Friends and Crocodiles* takes place at Lizzie's wedding. She has had a long, full and tumultuous relationship with Paul whom she, at the end of the section, notices has gate-crashed; provoking an immediate emotional response in her. See your personalized Paul. Place significant people or events on the sections of your mental roundabout, spin it around at varying speeds, record yourself and playback.

PAUL, OLIVER *and* BUTTERWORTH *approach the entrance to the marquee, keeping to the shadows, glancing at the reception through a flap. We see* LIZZIE *sitting with* RALPH *at the centre of the table, surrounded by flowers, with* SNEATH *next to them as the best man and* COYLE *near* LIZZIE *too.* SNEATH, *thinking* PAUL *has left, is looking much more relaxed. He stands up and taps the microphone.*

SNEATH: Any moment the speeches will be descending, so scrape those plates … Lick those bowls … !

As SNEATH *is saying this* LIZZIE *suddenly looks up and sees* PAUL *for the first time. She goes pale, immediately stops talking, their eyes meet. Then* LIZZIE *turns away to her next-door neighbour.*

See https://vimeo.com/251802093 for a demonstration.

Keep it simmering

If you are auditioning for the part of a psychopath who is just about to kill his next victims in a bloody rampage, you don't want to walk into the room in character as it may unnerve the auditioners. However, you will need to hit your level of intensity immediately when appropriate and called for. This may be tricky to achieve from a standing start, but technique will help.

You cook a beautiful and complex stew, blending together the finest fresh ingredients and leave it simmering on the backburner to be eaten later. Then, when it is time to serve, you crank up the heat to boiling point and go for it.

The process is the same with the audition. You have done your preparation and your character is ready. In the same way as when you worked on sense memory and affective memory in earlier chapters, you have picked images, sounds, tastes, sensations and smells to trigger the desired levels in the scene. It is important to make these triggers simple and easy to access to help you snap into the mental, physical and emotional state for the scene – maybe by using the sound of the air conditioning unit in the room if it is a kitchen or street, or the bland painted walls if it is a police cell? And when the moment of *action* arrives, you flash on these triggers to hit the spot.

EXERCISE

- Record yourself doing an affective memory exercise on anger whilst constantly moving your head, fingers and toes. Notice how long it takes and the ease of access or otherwise to any emotion.
- Now do the same thing but keep still. Allow your 20 per cent inner actor to notice the pressure build up inside you.
- Watch them both back and notice any difference.

25
WRAPPING IT UP

My aim in writing this book was to encourage you to get out of your own way and into the life of another; removing the pressure by eliminating unnecessary burdens to allow you the freedom to create truthful and unique characters and performances. What is important now is for you to reflect on what works for you and put any helpful tips and tools into practice.

Consider your ideal life, the career you want and the parts you want to play as all being achievable.

See success as a journey not a destination.

By committing to being as good as you can be in your chosen profession you can help change people's lives, their views on the world and the way they interact with it and each other.

You can help them commit to the stories you tell by believing them yourself.

Build interesting, colourful, real and believable characters. Use your experiences, emotions, senses and imagination. Rediscover your inner child and play. Make things up. Work hard, enjoy it and practise, practise, practise!

The truth starts with you, but it starts with an unblemished and obstacle-free you. Know who you are so you can know others. Know others so you can affect others.

APPENDICES

Appendix 1 – Values table

Value	What the word means to me	Currently honouring/10	Ways to increase the score to 10
1.			
2.			
3.			
4.			
5.			
6.			
7.			
8.			
9.			
10.			

Appendix 2 – Sample completed values table

Value	What the word means to me	Currently honouring/10	Ways to increase the score to 10
1. Integrity	Being honest. Standing up for myself and all my other values.	8	Increase the scores below by 1 point each.
2. Variety	Need to do lots of different work and activities to prevent boredom.	6	Go down to three days a week in my day job and join a clowning class. Walk home from the station a different way every day.
3. Creativity	Expression, spontaneity and newness. A deep need in me.	5	As above and spend the other two days working on characters.
4. Reciprocity	2-way street. People give back like I give back. Balance and generosity.	7	Tell my friend that she treats me like her chauffeur.
5. Personal Development	Learning and growing as a person. Expanding skills and having more to do.	4	Learn French through an app every day for half an hour and brush up my horse-riding skills at a local stable on Saturdays.
6. Determination	The will and drive to get things done and make a success of life.	3	Draw up a plan for my career and stick to it. Start with the plan and do one step at a time.
7. Justice	Fairness and equality. Class and race. Disadvantage versus privilege.	7	Join local social justice action group next Thursday.
8. Identity	Who am I and where do I come from?	6	Ask my grandpa where he came from and when and why he came to this country. Research heritage and join community group.
9. Family	Total and unconditional support and honesty.	8	Call my mum tonight!
10. Love	Unidentifiable and unmanageable personal connection. Physical and spiritual.	9	Tell my partner and my family that I love them and back it up by sending flowers.

Appendix 3 – Wheel of life

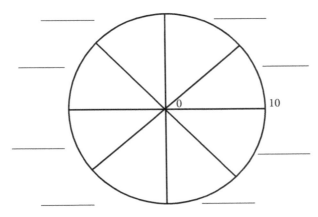

Figure 1 Wheel of life.

INSTRUCTIONS

Give a heading to each section of the wheel which represents a meaningful category in your life; such as career, money, personal development, home and physical environment, fun and recreation, friends and family, significant other, health. Give a score out of ten to each as to how fulfilled you are with the category.

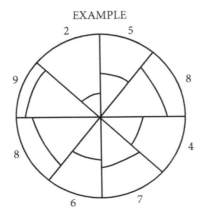

Figure 2 Example of wheel of life.

Appendix 4 – Meet your captain

If you could make yourself as comfortable as possible, and if you'd like to place your feet flat on the floor and close your eyes, please do so. And just breathe gently in and out … and as you are breathing gently in and out maybe your blood pressure is lowering, and your heart rate is decreasing … just breathing gently in and out … and as you are breathing in and out maybe you are beginning to feel a little more relaxed … that's right … still breathing gently in and out … and your blood pressure may be lowering, and your heart rate may be decreasing, and you may be feeling a little more relaxed … now focus on an image, it can be any image, an object, a colour anything you like … still breathing gently in and out … and now you can focus on a sound, it can be any sound … in a moment, I'm going to ask if you would like to take a journey, a journey to a place, a special place to you, your special place … if you'd like to take this journey now please do so in any way you wish, in your own unique way … and when you arrive in your special place, notice what is around you … notice what you see … maybe you can hear something … maybe you can touch something or feel something against your skin … maybe you can smell something … maybe you can taste something in your mouth …

This is your special place. A place which is special to you. One which you can always return to whenever you need or want. Your special place …

Now you hear someone approaching. It is your captain, and as your captain approaches notice:

- What stands out about them?
- What does the energy of your captain feel like?
- What's it like being with them?

This is the leader within you. This is your inner authority. Your captain loves you completely and unconditionally and believes in you completely and without question.

Greet one another and notice what it's like … and find a place to be with each other for a conversation, make yourself comfortable and ask the following questions:

- What is important for me to know about you?
- What is your role in my life?
- What do you want for me?
- What do you know about my life purpose?
- What is standing in my way?

- What name shall I call you by?
- How can I connect easily with your wisdom and strength?

Now they have a gift for you. Receive their gift.

- Notice what it is.
- What do you notice about it?
- Ask them what they would like you to know about this gift?

Now the meeting is coming to a close and it's time to thank each other, knowing that your captain will always be with you whenever you choose. They have always been here, and you now have access to them in a new and conscious way. Your Captain is here to support you.

And once again, in your special place, maybe you can taste something in your mouth … maybe you can smell something … maybe you can touch something or feel something against your skin … maybe you can hear something … and see something … and if you'd like to take a journey back to your physical place here … and once again focus on a sound, any sound … and on an image, it can be an object, a colour, anything you wish …

And when you're ready, if you'd like, you can open your eyes and bring yourselves back to the here and now.

Appendix 5 – Characteristics, history and experiences

CHILDHOOD AND FAMILY

full name
place and date of birth
class status of family
names and occupations of parents
place or places where childhood spent
any nick-name during childhood
relationship with parents
are parents still living
if sibling(s), names, gender and relative age
if sibling(s), emotional relationship with them
recollection of early childhood – e.g. happy, relaxed, turbulent, lonely …
recollection of adolescence
did the family move home; if so, how many times, why and where to?
national environment during childhood
social environment during childhood
cultural environment during childhood
religious environment during childhood
political environment during childhood
memories of childhood: houses, bedrooms, kitchens, classrooms, gardens …
memories of childhood: favourite toys, games, books, films, TV shows
memories of any outstandingly happy events during pre-adulthood life
memories of any outstandingly unhappy events during pre-adulthood life

EDUCATION

type and location of primary, secondary and further education
were schools mixed or single sex?
preferred subjects
preferred sports
other activities at school
friends at school
teachers at school
status among peers at school
successes and/or failures at school

early training and/or developed skills – music, craft, sport
any hobbies, interests, clubs, part time employment, ambitions, pets?
sexual awareness, development and/or experience

EARLY ADULT LIFE

if university, was there a gap year first? If so how was it spent?
if university, which one?
which subject(s) were read?
other activities at university
friends at university
tutors at university
status among peers at university
successes and/or failures at university
if other further education what subject(s) were studied?
other activities during further education
friends during further education
tutors during further education
status among peers during further education
successes and/or failures during further education
expressed life-plans and/or ambitions
any nickname?
memories of: bedrooms, kitchens, classrooms, gardens ...
memories of early adult life: books, pop groups, films, TV shows ...
memories of any outstandingly happy events during pre-adult life
memories of any outstandingly unhappy events during pre-adult life

CAREER

trade or profession
casual, freelance, contract, permanent staff
field of activity – commercial, industrial, service, science, the arts ...
how long after end of education before first job?
experience during first job
first job satisfaction, financial reward, social environment, prospects
further employment history
changes in status
periods of unemployment
current employment: responsibilities, status, colleagues, recognition ...
friendships/relationships derived from working life

PERSONAL LIFE

partnership history during adult life
if in a current relationship, full name and age of partner
how permanent, how long, how successful?
engaged? married? separating?
if children, names, ages, schools or occupations
sexual satisfaction
cultural compatibility
social compatibility
a team or two individuals?
prospects
residence – house, flat, large, small, garden, owned, mortgaged, rented …
environment – town, country, seaside, remote, up/down market …
hobbies, pastimes, charitable work
leisure activities shared or alone?
ongoing relationship with children
ongoing relationship with parents
ongoing relationship with siblings

BELIEFS AND OPINIONS

religious
moral
social
politics
green issues …
morality
extra-marital partnerships and sexual experience
observance of the law
attitude to petty crime
charity

BEHAVIOURAL TENDENCIES

tolerance/intolerance of irritants – barking dogs, loud voices, stupidity …
concern – offering to help a pram up a step …
compassion – 'what must it be like to be that African child' …
liberal – 'young hooligans aren't criminals; they're victims of neglect' …
reactionary – 'so, build more prisons' …
introverted – withdrawn, distant, unforthcoming …
extrovert – outgoing, co-operative, attention seeking

active – building, improving, transforming …
passive – complacent, self-satisfied, insular …
physically brave/physically cowardly
morally brave/morally cowardly
honest/dissembling

HOPES AND FEARS

personal ambitions – high status, recognition, celebrity, power, revenge
hopes – self-respect, security, peace, happy marriage, successful children …
fears – embarrassment, disdain, failure, illness, death …

BURDENS

guilt
mannerisms
habits
secrets
regrets …
weaknesses
dishonesty
indecision
phobias
laziness
selfishness …

STRENGTHS

determination
commitment
loyalty
honesty
love …

CURRENTLY

emotional stability
financial stability
physical condition
living at home
living in house, flat, homeless

living with parents
living with partner and children
relationship with partner
which side of the bed
relationship with friends/colleagues/associates
relationship with parents
relationship with siblings
relationship with children
any guilty secrets
any secret plans
any major hope/unfulfilled ambition
any major worry/fear
any suppressed emotion – anger/sorrow/lust …
daily routine
free time/fun time
holidays …
recent important events – rows, birthdays, accidents, illnesses, triumphs …
regular newspaper(s)/magazine …
book/novel …
favourite TV comedian …
A la carte, table d'hôte, Chinese, fish and chips …
Brahms, Elton John, folk, Johnny Cash, R&B, Hip Hop, 50 Cent …
Constable, Turner, Van Gogh, Picasso, Warhol, Freud, Hockney, Emin …
bicycle, motor bike, car …
cats or dogs?
wine, beer, coke or orange juice?
Saville Row, M&S, tracksuit, jeans, Oxfam …
and …

Appendix 6 – Meet your character

If you could make yourself as comfortable as possible, and if you'd like to place your feet flat on the floor and close your eyes, please do so. And just breathe gently in and out … and as you are breathing gently in and out maybe your blood pressure is lowering, and your heart rate is decreasing … just breathing gently in and out … and as you are breathing in and out maybe you are beginning to feel a little more relaxed … that's right … still breathing gently in and out … and your blood pressure may be lowering, and your heart rate may be decreasing, and you may be feeling a little more relaxed … now focus on an image, it can be any image, an object, a colour anything you like … still breathing gently in and out … and now you can focus on a sound, it can be any sound … in a moment, I'm going to ask if you would like to take a journey, a journey to a place, a special place to you, your special place … if you'd like to take this journey now please do so in any way you wish, in your own unique way … and when you arrive in your special place, notice what is around you … notice what you see … maybe you can hear something … maybe you can touch something or feel something against your skin … maybe you can smell something … maybe you can taste something in your mouth …

This is your special place. A place which is special to you. One which you can always return to whenever you need or want. Your special place …

Now you hear someone approaching. It is your character. And as they approach notice what they look like … what stands out about them? … notice what their energy feels like … what's it like being with them? … greet one another and notice what it's like …

Now find a place to be with each other for a conversation and make yourselves comfortable … and ask the following questions:

- What is important for me to know about you?
- What is your role in life?
- What do you want?
- What is your life purpose?
- What is standing in your way?
- What is your biggest secret?
- What name shall I call you by?
- How can I connect easily with you?

Now they have a gift for you. Receive their gift.

- What is it?

- What do you notice about it?
- Ask them what they would like you to know about this gift?

And if you'd like to ask them any other question please do so …

And now the meeting is coming to a close. It is time to thank each other knowing that, as night follows day, you have access to them in a new and conscious way and that you can access them whenever you choose.

And once again, in your place, maybe you can taste something in your mouth … maybe you can smell something … maybe you can touch something or feel something against your skin … maybe you can hear something … and see something … and if you'd like to take a journey back to this place … and once again focus on a sound, any sound … and on an image, it can be an object, a colour, anything you wish … and when you're ready, if you'd like, you can open your eyes and bring yourselves back to the here and now.

REFERENCES

Adler, S. (2000). *Stella Adler – The Art of Acting*. New York: Applause Books.

AZQuotes. (n.d.). Meryl Streep Quotes. http://www.azquotes.com/quote/1185498.

Ballard, J. G. (1984). What I Believe. *Interzone*, no. 8 (Summer).

Benton, R. (Director). (1979). *Kramer vs Kramer* [Motion Picture].

Benton, R. (Director). (2003). *The Human Stain* [Motion Picture].

Britten, B. (2015). *From Stage to Screen*. London: Bloomsbury/Methuen.

Brown, B. (n.d.). *The Power of Vulnerability*. Ted Talks. https://www.ted.com/talks/brene_brown_on_vulnerability/transcript/.

Bryan Cranston's Advice to Aspiring Actors. (2013). YouTube, 27 September. https://www.youtube.com/watch?v=v1WiCGq-PcY/.

Caine, M. (2000). *Acting in Film*. New York: Applause Books.

Cianfrance, D. (Director). (2010). *Blue Valentine* [Motion Picture].

Clance, P. and Imes, S. (1978). The Imposter Phenomenon in High Achieving Women: Dynamics and Therapeutic Intervention. *Psychotherapy: Theory, Research and Practice*, vol. 15, no. 3.

Columbus, C. (Director). (1998). *Stepmom* [Motion Picture].

Coppola, F. F. (Director). (1972). *The Godfather* [Motion Picture].

Coppola, F. F. (Director). (1974). *The Godfather II* [Motion Picture].

Coppola, F. F. (Director). (1990). *The Godfather III* [Motion Picture].

Darwin, C. (1872). *Expression of the Emotions in Man and Animals*. London: John Murray.

Dotson Rader, P. (1998). How Mrs Big Brain Became a Star. *Parade*, 11 October.

Eby, D. (2009). Gain a Stronger Acting Performance without Fraud Feelings. *EzineArticles*, 19 April. http://ezinearticles.com/?Gain-a-Stronger-Acting-Performance-Without-Fraud-Feelings&id=2242220/.

Gevinson, T. (2013). I Want It to Be Worth It: An Interview With Emma Watson. *Rookie*, 27 May. http://www.rookiemag.com/2013/05/emma-watson-interview/2/.

Gladwell, M. (2008). *The Outliers: The Story of Success*. New York: Little, Brown and Co.

Grotowski, J. (1975). *Towards a Poor Theatre*. London: Bloomsbury.

Hollywood Reporter. (2006). Dialogue: Anthony Hopkins. *Backstage,* 18 January. https://www.backstage.com/news/dialogue-anthony-hopkins/.

Horowitz, A. (Director). (2002–15). *Foyle's War* [Television Series].

IMDB. (n.d.). Paul Newman. http://www.imdb.com/name/nm0000056/.

Johnson, Z. and Malkin, M. (2016). Renée Zellweger Reflects on Her Return to Acting and Suffering from Imposter Syndrome. *E! News*, 31 August.

Kazan, E. (Director). (1951). *A Streetcar Named Desire* [Motion Picture].

Kimsey House, H. et al. (2011). *Co-Active Coaching*, 3rd edition. London: Nicholas Brealey.

Kubrick, S. (Director). (1980). *The Shining* [Motion Picture].

Lee, C. (2004). A Hard Look at Himself. *LA Times*, 14 November. http://articles.latimes.com/2004/nov/14/entertainment/ca-cheadle14/.

Lennon, J. (1980). Beautiful Boy [Recorded by J. Lennon].

Longwell, D. (1987). *Sanford Meisner on Acting*. London: Random House.

Luhrmann, B. (Director). (2013). *The Great Gatsby* [Motion Picture].

Marsh, J. (Director). (2014). *The Theory of Everything* [Motion Picture].

Mehrabian, A. (1971). *Silent Messages*. Belmont, CA: Wadsworth.

Mullan, P. (Director). (2002). *The Magdalene Sisters* [Motion Picture].

Obst, L. (2000). Kate Winslet: A Heavenly Creature Who Breaks All the Formulas. *Interview Magazine*, November.

Pavlov, I. (1904). *The Nobel Prize in Physiology and Medicine*. Sweden: Nobel Media.

Poliakoff, S. (2005). *Friends and Crocodiles*. London: Bloomsbury.

Sagan, C. (1980). *Cosmos*. London: Random House.

Schlesinger, J. (Director). (1969). *Midnight Cowboy* [Motion Picture].

Scorsese, M. (Director). (1976). *Taxi Driver* [Motion Picture].

Shorten, K. (2013). High-achievers Suffering from 'Imposter Syndrome'. *News.com.au*, 10 December: http://www.news.com.au/finance/highachievers-suffering-from-imposter-syndrome/news-story/9e2708a0d0b7590994be28bb6f47b9bc/.

Shortlist. (n.d.). Anthony Hopkins Interview. https://www.shortlist.com/entertainment/anthony-hopkins-interview/98274/.

Smith, L. (2017). Why Women Experience 'Impostor Syndrome' – and How to Beat it. *Cosmopolitan*, 18 August. http://www.cosmopolitan.com/uk/reports/a12029501/impostor-syndrome-women-what-is-it-how-to-beat-it/.

Sorkin, A. (Director). (1999–2006). *West Wing* [Television Series].

Spielberg, S. (Director). (1975). *Jaws* [Motion Picture].

Sturges, J. (Director). (1960). *The Magnificent Seven* [Motion Picture].

Wells, J. (Director). (2013). *August: Osage County* [Motion Picture].

Wilde, O. (1891). *The Soul of Man under Socialism*. Whitefish, MT: Kessinger Publishing.

Wiseman, R. (2004). *Did You Spot the Gorilla*. London: Random House.

LIST OF VIDEO
AND AUDIO LINKS

Chapter 2 – Values and Fulfilment – **https://vimeo.com/251793351**
Chapter 3 – Saboteurs and Limiting Beliefs – AUDIO FILE ONLY –
   https://vimeo.com/251793473
Chapter 11 – Emotions – Affective memory – **https://vimeo.com/251793609**
Chapter 13 – Listening – **https://vimeo.com/251793757**
Chapter 15 – Lines and Learning them – **https://vimeo.com/251793902**
Chapter 16 – Adjusting Your Vocal Levels – **https://vimeo.com/251794174**
Chapter 19 – Truth – **https://vimeo.com/251794286**
Chapter 20 – Senses and Sense Memory – the breakfast drink –
   https://vimeo.com/251794362
Chapter 20 – Senses and Sense Memory – Mirror – **https://vimeo.com/251795537**
Chapter 20 – Senses and Sense Memory – Sun and monologue, then rain and
   monologue – **https://vimeo.com/251795623**
Chapter 21 – Thinking and the Inner Monologue (part 1) – an inner monologue
   exercise – **https://vimeo.com/251797118**
Chapter 21 – Thinking and the Inner Monologue (part 2) – thinking strong
   thoughts – **https://vimeo.com/251797270**
Chapter 23 – Meet Your Character – AUDIO FILE ONLY –
   https://vimeo.com/251801989
Chapter 24 – Mind, Body and Soul – the roundabout – **https://vimeo.com/251802093**
Chapter 24 – Mind, Body and Soul – actor demonstration of doubling and doubling
   again – **https://vimeo.com/251802351**

INDEX